Congressional Research Service
Informing the legislative debate since 1914 _____

Navy Force Structure and Shipbuilding Plans: Background and Issues for Congress

Ronald O'Rourke
Specialist in Naval Affairs

June 20, 2014

Congressional Research Service

7-5700

www.crs.gov

RL32665

Summary

The Navy's proposed FY2015 budget requests funding for the procurement of seven new battle force ships (i.e., ships that count against the Navy's goal for achieving and maintaining a fleet of 306 ships). The seven ships include two Virginia-class attack submarines, two DDG-51 class Aegis destroyers, and three Littoral Combat Ships (LCSs). The Navy's proposed FY2015-FY2019 five-year shipbuilding plan includes a total of 44 ships, compared to a total of 41 ships in the FY2014-FY2018 five-year shipbuilding plan.

The planned size of the Navy, the rate of Navy ship procurement, and the prospective affordability of the Navy's shipbuilding plans have been matters of concern for the congressional defense committees for the past several years. The Navy's FY2015 30-year (FY2014-FY2044) shipbuilding plan, like many previous Navy 30-year shipbuilding plans, does not include enough ships to fully support all elements of the Navy's 306-ship goal over the entire 30-year period. In particular, the Navy projects that the fleet would experience a shortfall in amphibious ships from FY2015 through FY2017, a shortfall in small surface combatants from FY2015 through FY2027, and a shortfall in attack submarines from FY2025 through FY2034.

In its October 2013 report on the cost of the FY2014 30-year shipbuilding plan, the Congressional Budget Office (CBO) estimates that the plan would cost an average of $19.3 billion per year in constant FY2013 dollars to implement, or about 15% more than the Navy estimates. CBO's estimate is about 6% higher than the Navy's estimate for the first 10 years of the plan, about 14% higher than the Navy's estimate for the second 10 years of the plan, and about 26% higher than the Navy's estimate for the final 10 years of the plan. Some of the difference between CBO's estimate and the Navy's estimate, particularly in the latter years of the plan, is due to a difference between CBO and the Navy in how to treat inflation in Navy shipbuilding.

Potential issues for Congress in reviewing the Navy's proposed FY2015 shipbuilding budget, its proposed FY2015-FY2019 five-year shipbuilding plan, and its FY2015 30-year (FY2015-FY2044) shipbuilding plan include the following:

- the Navy's proposal to defer until FY2016 a decision on whether to proceed with the mid-life nuclear refueling overhaul of the aircraft carrier *George Washington* (CVN-73);

- the Navy's proposal to put 11 of its 22 Aegis cruisers into some form of reduced operating status starting in FY2015, and then return them to service years from now;

- the Navy's proposal to retire all 10 of its remaining Oliver Hazard Perry (FFG-7) class frigates in FY2015;

- the Navy's proposal to modify the rules for what ships to include in the count of the number of battle force ships in the Navy;

- the potential impact on the size of the Navy of limiting DOD spending in FY2013-FY2021 to the levels set forth in the Budget Control Act of 2011, as amended;

- the appropriate future size and structure of the Navy in light of budgetary and strategic considerations; and

- the affordability of the 30-year shipbuilding plan.

Funding levels and legislative activity on individual Navy shipbuilding programs are tracked in detail in other CRS reports.

Contents

Tables

Appendixes

Contacts

Introduction

This report provides background information and presents potential issues for Congress concerning the Navy's ship force-structure goals and shipbuilding plans. The planned size of the Navy, the rate of Navy ship procurement, and the prospective affordability of the Navy's shipbuilding plans have been matters of concern for the congressional defense committees for the past several years. Decisions that Congress makes on Navy shipbuilding programs can substantially affect Navy capabilities and funding requirements, and the U.S. shipbuilding industrial base.

Background

Navy's Ship Force Structure Goal

January 2013 Goal for Fleet of 306 Ships

On January 31, 2013, in response to Section 1015 of the FY2013 National Defense Authorization Act (H.R. 4310/P.L. 112-239 of January 2, 2013), the Navy submitted to Congress a report presenting a goal for achieving and maintaining a fleet of 306 ships, consisting of certain types and quantities of ships.[1] The goal for a 306-ship fleet is the result of a force structure assessment (FSA) that the Navy completed in 2012.

306-Ship Goal Reflects 2012 Strategic Guidance and Projected DOD Spending Shown in FY2013 and FY2014 Budget Submissions

The 2012 FSA and the resulting 306-ship plan reflect the defense strategic guidance document that the Administration presented in January 2012[2] and the associated projected levels of Department of Defense (DOD) spending shown in the FY2013 and FY2014 budget submissions. DOD officials have stated that if planned levels of DOD spending are reduced below what is shown in these budget submissions, the defense strategy set forth in the January 2012 strategic guidance document might need to be changed. Such a change, Navy officials have indicated, could lead to the replacement of the 306-ship plan of January 2013 with a new plan.

Goal for Fleet of 306 Ships Compared to Earlier Goals

Table 1 compares the 306-ship goal to earlier Navy ship force structure plans.

---

[1] Department of the Navy, *Report to Congress [on] Navy Combatant Vessel Force Structure Requirement*, January 2013, 3 pp. The cover letters for the report were dated January 31, 2013.

[2] For more on this document, see CRS Report R42146, *Assessing the January 2012 Defense Strategic Guidance (DSG): In Brief*, by Catherine Dale and Pat Towell.

Table 1. Current 306 Ship Force Structure Goal Compared to Earlier Goals

Ship type	306-ship plan of January 2013	~310-316 ship plan of March 2012	Revised 313-ship plan of September 2011	Changes to February 2006 313-ship plan announced through mid-2011	February 2006 Navy plan for 313-ship fleet	Early-2005 Navy plan for fleet of 260-325 ships		2002-2004 Navy plan for 375-ship Navy[a]	2001 QDR plan for 310-ship Navy
						260-ships	325-ships		
Ballistic missile submarines (SSBNs)	12[b]	12-14[b]	12[b]	12[b]	14	14	14	14	14
Cruise missile submarines (SSGNs)	0[c]	0-4[c]	4[c]	0[c]	4	4	4	4	2 or 4[d]
Attack submarines (SSNs)	48	~48	48	48	48	37	41	55	55
Aircraft carriers	11[e]	11[e]	11[e]	11[e]	11[f]	10	11	12	12
Cruisers and destroyers	88	~90	94	94[g]	88	67	92	104	116
Frigates	0	0	0	0	0	0	0	0	
Littoral Combat Ships (LCSs)	52	~55	55	55	55	63	82	56	0
Amphibious ships	33	~32	33	33[h]	31	17	24	37	36
MPF(F) ships[i]	0[i]	0[i]	0[i]	0[i]	12[i]	14[i]	20[i]	0[i]	0[i]
Combat logistics (resupply) ships	29	~29	30	30	30	24	26	42	34
Dedicated mine warfare ships	0	0	0	0	0	0	0	26[k]	16
Joint High Speed Vessels (JHSVs)	10[l]	10[l]	10[l]	21[l]	3	0	0	0	0
Other[m]	23	~23	16	24[n]	17	10	11	25	25
Total battle force ships	**306**	**~310-316**	**313**	**328**	**313**	**260**	**325**	**375**	**310 or 312**

Sources: Table prepared by CRS based on U.S. Navy data.

Note: QDR is Quadrennial Defense Review. The "~" symbol means approximately and signals that the number in question may be refined as a result of the Naval Force Structure Assessment currently in progress.

a. Initial composition. Composition was subsequently modified.

b. The Navy plans to replace the 14 current Ohio-class SSBNs with a new class of 12 next-generation SSBNs. For further discussion, see CRS Report R41129, *Navy Ohio Replacement (SSBN[X]) Ballistic Missile Submarine Program: Background and Issues for Congress*, by Ronald O'Rourke.

c. Although the Navy plans to continue operating its four SSGNs until they reach retirement age in the late 2020s, the Navy does not plan to replace these ships when they retire. This situation can be expressed in a table like this one with either a 4 or a zero.

d. The report on the 2001 QDR did not mention a specific figure for SSGNs. The Administration's proposed FY2001 DOD budget requested funding to support the conversion of two available Trident SSBNs into SSGNs, and the retirement of two other Trident SSBNs. Congress, in marking up this request, supported a plan to convert all four available SSBNs into SSGNs.

e. With congressional approval, the goal has been temporarily be reduced to 10 carriers for the period between the retirement of the carrier *Enterprise* (CVN-65) in December 2012 and entry into service of the carrier *Gerald R. Ford* (CVN-78), currently scheduled for September 2015.

f. For a time, the Navy characterized the goal as 11 carriers in the nearer term, and eventually 12 carriers.

g. The 94-ship goal was announced by the Navy in an April 2011 report to Congress on naval force structure and missile defense.

h. The Navy acknowledged that meeting a requirement for being able to lift the assault echelons of 2.0 Marine Expeditionary Brigades (MEBs) would require a minimum of 33 amphibious ships rather than the 31 ships shown in the February 2006 plan. For further discussion, see CRS Report RL34476, *Navy LPD-17 Amphibious Ship Procurement: Background, Issues, and Options for Congress*, by Ronald O'Rourke.

i. Today's Maritime Prepositioning Force (MPF) ships are intended primarily to support Marine Corps operations ashore, rather than Navy combat operations, and thus are not counted as Navy battle force ships. The planned MPF (Future) ships, however, would have contributed to Navy combat capabilities (for example, by supporting Navy aircraft operations). For this reason, the ships in the planned MPF(F) squadron were counted by the Navy as battle force ships. The planned MPF(F) squadron was subsequently restructured into a different set of initiatives for enhancing the existing MPF squadrons; the Navy no longer plans to acquire an MPF(F) squadron.

j. The Navy no longer plans to acquire an MPF(F) squadron. The Navy, however, has procured or plans to procure some of the ships that were previously planned for the squadron—specifically, TAKE-1 class cargo ships, and Mobile Landing Platform (MLP)/Afloat Forward Staging Base (AFSB) ships. These ships are included in the total shown for "Other" ships.

k. The figure of 26 dedicated mine warfare ships included 10 ships maintained in a reduced mobilization status called Mobilization Category B. Ships in this status are not readily deployable and thus do not count as battle force ships. The 375-ship proposal thus implied transferring these 10 ships to a higher readiness status.

l. Totals shown include 5 ships transferred from the Army to the Navy and operated by the Navy primarily for the performance of Army missions.

m. This category includes, among other things, command ships and support ships.

n. The increase in this category from 17 ships under the February 2006 313-ship plan to 24 ships under the apparent 328-ship goal included the addition of one TAGOS ocean surveillance ship and the transfer into this category of six ships—three modified TAKE-1 class cargo ships, and three Mobile Landing Platform (MLP) ships—that were previously intended for the planned (but now canceled) MPF(F) squadron.

Navy's Five-Year and 30-Year Shipbuilding Plans

Five-Year (FY2015-FY2019) Shipbuilding Plan

Table 2 shows the Navy's FY2015 five-year (FY2015-FY2019) shipbuilding plan.

Table 2. Navy FY2014 Five-Year (FY2015-FY2019) Shipbuilding Plan

(Battle force ships—i.e., ships that count against 306-ship goal)

Ship type	FY15	FY16	FY17	FY18	FY19	Total
Ford (CVN-78) class aircraft carrier				1		1
Virginia (SSN-774) class attack submarine	2	2	2	2	2	10
Arleigh Burke (DDG-51) class destroyer	2	2	2	2	2	10
Littoral Combat Ship (LCS)	3	3	3	3	2	14
LHA(R) amphibious assault ship			1			1
Fleet tug (TATF)			2	1	1	4
Mobile Landing Platform (MLP)/Afloat Forward Staging Base (AFSB)			1			1
TAO(X) oiler		1		1	1	3
TOTAL	**7**	**8**	**11**	**10**	**8**	**44**

Source: FY2015 Navy budget submission.

Notes: The MLP/AFSB is a variant of the MLP with additional features permitting it to serve in the role of an AFSB. The Navy proposes to fund the TATFs and TAO(X)s through the National Defense Sealift Fund (NDSF) and the other ships through the Navy's shipbuilding account, known formally as the Shipbuilding and Conversion, Navy (SCN) appropriation account.

Observations that can be made about the Navy's proposed FY2015 five-year (FY2015-FY2019) shipbuilding plan include the following:

- **Total of 44 ships.** The plan includes a total of 44 ships, compared to a total of 41 ships in the FY2014-FY2018 five-year shipbuilding plan.

- **Average of 8.8 ships per year.** The plan includes an average of 8.8 battle force ships per year. The steady-state replacement rate for a fleet of 306 ships with an average service life of 35 years is about 8.7 ships per year. In light of how the average shipbuilding rate since FY1993 has been substantially below 8.7 ships per year (see **Appendix D**), shipbuilding supporters for some time have wanted to increase the shipbuilding rate to a steady rate of 10 or more battle force ships per year.

- **DDG-51 destroyers and Virginia-class submarines being procured under MYP arrangements.** The 10 DDG-51 destroyers to be procured in FY2013-FY2017 and the 10 Virginia-class attack submarines to be procured in FY2014-FY2018 are being procured under multiyear procurement (MYP) contracts.[3]

- **Navy is requesting three rather than four LCSs for FY2015.** LCSs are being procured under a pair of block buy contracts covering the years FY2010-FY2015. These two contracts call for a total of four LCSs in FY2015. The Navy, however, is requesting funding for the procurement of three LCSs in FY2015. If three LCSs are funded in FY2015, one of the two LCS block buy contracts would not be fully implemented in its final year.

- **Start of LX(R) amphibious ship procurement deferred to FY2020.** The FY2015-FY2019 five-year shipbuilding plan defers the procurement of the first LX(R) amphibious ship to FY2020, compared to FY2019 in the FY2014-FY2018 plan, FY2018 in the FY2013-FY2017 plan, and FY2017 in the FY2012-FY2016 plan. In each of these five-year plans, the lead LX(R) ship was scheduled one year beyond the end of the five-year period.

- **MLP/AFSB ship added to FY2017.** The FY2015-FY2019 five-year shipbuilding plan adds an MLP/AFSB (Mobile Landing Platform/Afloat Forward Staging Base) ship in FY2017. This ship, not previously planned, would likely be built by General Dynamics/National Steel and Shipbuilding Company (GD/NASSCO), the builder of prior MLP/AFSB ships. In addition to providing a platform that would help the Navy meet certain operational needs, adding this ship to the shipbuilding plan might help the Navy ensure strong competition for two other Navy ship programs—the TAO(X) oiler program, the first ship of which is to be procured in FY2016, and the LX(R) amphibious ship program, the first ship of which is to be procured in FY2020.[4]

---

[3] For more on MYP contracting, see CRS Report R41909, *Multiyear Procurement (MYP) and Block Buy Contracting in Defense Acquisition: Background and Issues for Congress*, by Ronald O'Rourke and Moshe Schwartz.

[4] NASSCO could be a bidder for either or both of the TAO(X) and LX(R) programs. From a competition perspective, the added FY2017 MLP/AFSB ship might be viewed as a Navy signal to NASSCO that the Navy would not necessarily (continued...)

30-Year (FY2015-FY2044) Shipbuilding Plan

Table 3 shows the Navy's FY2015 30-year (FY2015-FY2044) shipbuilding plan.

Table 3. Navy FY2015 30-Year (FY2015-FY2044) Shipbuilding Plan

FY	CVN	LSC	SSC	SSN	SSBN	AWS	CLF	Supt	Total
15		2	3	2					7
16		2	3	2			I		8
17		2	3	2		I		3	11
18	I	2	3	2			I	I	10
19		2	2	2			I	I	8
20		2	3	2		I	I	2	11
21		2	3	I	I		I		8
22		2	3	2		I	I	2	11
23	I	2	3	I			I	3	11
24		2	3	2	I	2	I	2	13
25		2	3	I			I	I	8
26		2		2	I	I	I		7
27		2		I	I		I		5
28	I	2		2	I	2	I	I	10
29		2		I	I	I	I	I	7
30		2	I	2	I	I	I	2	10
31		2		I	I	I	I	2	8
32		2	I	2	I	2	I	3	12
33	I	2		I	I	I	I	2	9
34		2	I	2	I	I		2	9
35		2	I	I	I				5
36		2		2		I			5
37		2	4	I					7
38	I	3	4	2					10
39		3	4	I					8
40		3	4	2		2			11
41		3	4	I					8
42		3	4	2		I			10
43	I	2	4	I			I		9
44		2	2	2		2			8

Source: FY2015 30-year (FY2015-FY2044) shipbuilding plan.

(...continued)

award NASSCO the TAO(X) program merely to provide a source work for NASSCO until the LX(R) competition (because NASSCO would likely receive the FY2017 MLP/AFSB), and consequently that NASSCO would need to submit a competitive bid for the TAO(X) program. By the same token, the added FY2017 MLP/AFSB ship might be viewed as a Navy signal to potential bidders for the LX(R) program other than NASSCO that if NASSCO were not awarded the TAO(X) program, NASSCO would still have enough work to be a strong bidder for the LX(R) program (again because NASSCO would likely receive the FY2017 MLP/AFSB), and consequently that LX(R) bidders other than NASSCO would face strong competition from NASSCO. Another potential implication from this perspective is that if NASSCO wins the TAO(X) competition, the Navy, other things held equal, might see less reason to retain the FY2017 MLP/AFSB in the shipbuilding plan.

Key: FY = Fiscal Year; **CVN** = aircraft carriers; **LSC** = surface combatants (i.e., cruisers and destroyers); **SSC** = small surface combatants (i.e., Littoral Combat Ships [LCSs]); **SSN** = attack submarines; **SSGN** = cruise missile submarines; **SSBN** = ballistic missile submarines; **AWS** = amphibious warfare ships; **CLF** = combat logistics force (i.e., resupply) ships; **Supt** = support ships.

In devising a 30-year shipbuilding plan to move the Navy toward its ship force-structure goal, key assumptions and planning factors include but are not limited to the following:

- ship service lives;

- estimated ship procurement costs;

- projected shipbuilding funding levels; and

- industrial-base considerations.

Navy's Projected Force Levels Under 30-Year Shipbuilding Plan

Table 4 shows the Navy's projection of ship force levels for FY2015-FY2044 that would result from implementing the FY2015 30-year (FY2015-FY2044) shipbuilding plan shown in **Table 3**.

As part of its FY2015 budget submission, the Navy is proposing to modify the rules for what ships to include in the count of the number of battle force ships in the Navy. In its FY2015 budget submission, the Navy has presented figures for projected Navy ship force levels using both the existing rules and the proposed modified rules. **Table 4** and **Table 6** show figures using both the existing rules and the proposed modified rules.

Table 4. Projected Force Levels Resulting from FY2015 30-Year (FY2015-FY2044) Shipbuilding Plan

Where two figures are shown, the first is the figure using existing rules for counting battle force ships, and the second is the figure using the Navy's proposed modified rules for counting battle force ships.

	CVN	LSC	SSC	SSN	SSGN	SSBN	AWS	CLF	Supt	Total
306 ship plan	11	88	52	48	0	12	33	29	33	306
FY15	10	85	19/26	54	4	14	30	29	29/32	274/284
FY16	11	88	23/30	53	4	14	31	29	27/30	280/290
FY17	11	90	27/34	50	4	14	32	29	29/32	286/296
FY18	11	92/91	31/38	52	4	14	33	29	29/32	295/304
FY19	11	93	35/40	51	4	14	33	29	31/34	301/309
FY20	11	95	36/37	49	4	14	33	29	33/36	304/308
FY21	11	96	36/33	49	4	14	33	29	32/35	304
FY22	11	97	38/36	48	4	14	33	29	32/35	306/307
FY23	12	98	39	49	4	14	33	29	33/36	311/314
FY24	12	98	41/40	48	4	14	34	29	33/36	313/315
FY25	11	98	43	47	4	14	34	29	34/37	314/317
FY26	11	97	46	45	2	14	36	29	34/37	314/317
FY27	11	99	49	44	1	13	35	29	34/37	315/318
FY28	11	100	52	41	0	13	36	29	34/37	316/319
FY29	11	98	52	41	0	12	35	29	34/37	312/315
FY30	11	95	52	41	0	11	35	29	34/37	308/311
FY31	11	91	52	43	0	11	34	29	34/36	305/307
FY32	11	89	52	43	0	10	34	29	35/37	303/305
FY33	11	88	52	45	0	10	35	29	35/37	305/307
FY34	11	86	52	46	0	10	34	29	35/37	303/305
FY35	11	87	52	48	0	10	32	29	35/37	304/306
FY36	11	88	52	49	0	10	32	29	35	306
FY37	11	90	52	51	0	10	33	29	34	310
FY38	11	91	52	50	0	10	33	29	35	311
FY39	11	92	52	51	0	10	33	29	34	312
FY40	10	90	52	51	0	10	32	29	34	308
FY41	10	89	52	51	0	11	33	29	34	309
FY42	10	87	52	52	0	12	32	29	34	308
FY43	10	84	52	52	0	12	31	29	34	304
FY44	10	83	52	52	0	12	31	29	34	303

Source: FY2015 30-year (FY2015-FY2044) shipbuilding plan.

Note: Figures for support ships include five JHSVs transferred from the Army to the Navy and operated by the Navy primarily for the performance of Army missions.

Key: **FY** = Fiscal Year; **CVN** = aircraft carriers; **LSC** = surface combatants (i.e., cruisers and destroyers); **SSC** = small surface combatants (i.e., frigates, Littoral Combat Ships [LCSs], and mine warfare ships); **SSN** = attack submarines; **SSGN** = cruise missile submarines; **SSBN** = ballistic missile submarines; **AWS** = amphibious warfare ships; **CLF** = combat logistics force (i.e., resupply) ships; **Supt** = support ships.

Observations that can be made about the Navy's FY2014 30-year (FY2014-FY2043) shipbuilding plan and resulting projected force levels included the following:

- **Total of 264 ships; average of about 8.8 per year.** The plan includes a total of 264 ships to be procured, two less than the number in the FY2014 30-year (FY2014-FY2043) shipbuilding plan. The total of 264 ships equates to an average of about 8.8 ships per year, which is slightly higher than the approximate average procurement rate (sometimes called the steady-state replacement rate) of about 8.7 ships per year that would be needed over the long run to achieve and maintain a fleet of 306 ships, assuming an average life of 35 years for Navy ships.

- **Proposed modified counting rules affect small surface combatants and support ships.** As can be seen in **Table 4**, the Navy's proposed modified rules for what ships to include in the count of the number of battle force ships (see "Proposal to Modify What Ships Are Included in the Count of Battle Force Ships" in "Oversight Issues for Congress for FY2015") would affect the reported figures for small surface combatants during the period FY2015-FY2024 and the reported figures for support ships during the period FY2015-FY2035.

- **Eleven cruisers proposed for some form of reduced operating status included in count.** As part of its FY2015 budget submission, the Navy is proposing to put 11 of its 22 Aegis cruisers into some form of reduced operating status starting in FY2015, and then return them to service years from now. The 11 cruisers proposed for some form of reduced operating status are included in the count of battle force ships shown in **Table 4** and **Table 6** during the years that they are in reduced operating status.

- **Projected shortfalls in amphibious ships, small surface combatants, and attack submarines.** The FY2015 30-year shipbuilding plan, like many previous Navy 30-year shipbuilding plans, does not include enough ships to fully support all elements of the Navy's 306-ship goal over the entire 30-year period. In particular, the Navy projects that the fleet would experience a shortfall in amphibious ships from FY2015 through FY2017, a shortfall in small surface combatants from FY2015 through FY2027, and a shortfall in attack submarines from FY2025 through FY2034.

- **Ballistic missile submarine force to be reduced temporarily to 10 boats.** As a result of a decision in the FY2013 budget to defer the scheduled procurement of the first Ohio replacement (SSBN[X]) ballistic missile submarine by two years, from FY2019 to FY2021, the ballistic missile submarine force is projected to drop to a total of 10 or 11 boats—one or two boats below the 12-boat SSBN force-level goal—during the period FY2029-FY2041. The Navy says this reduction is acceptable for meeting current strategic nuclear deterrence mission requirements, because none of the 10 or 11 boats during these years will be encumbered by long-term maintenance.[5]

---

[5] For further discussion of this issue, see CRS Report R41129, *Navy Ohio Replacement (SSBN[X]) Ballistic Missile Submarine Program: Background and Issues for Congress*, by Ronald O'Rourke.

Comparison of First 10 Years of 30-Year Plans

Table 5 and **Table 6** below show the first 10 years of planned annual ship procurement quantities and projected Navy force sizes in 30-year shipbuilding plans dating back to the first such plan, which was submitted in 2000 in conjunction with the FY2001 budget. By reading vertically down each column, one can see how the ship procurement quantity or Navy force size projected for a given fiscal year changed as that year drew closer to becoming the current budget year.

Table 5. Ship Procurement Quantities in First 10 Years of 30-Year Shipbuilding Plans

Years shown are fiscal years

FY of 30-year plan (year submitted)	01	02	03	04	05	06	07	08	09	10	11	12	13	14	15	16	17	18	19	20	21	22	23	24
FY01 plan (2000)	8	8	8	8	7	5	6	6	6	7														
FY02 plan (2001)		6	n/a	n/a	n/a	n/a	n/a	n/a	n/a	n/a	n/a													
FY03 plan (2002)			5	5	7	7	11	n/a	n/a	n/a	n/a	n/a												
FY04 plan (2003)				7	8	7	7	9	14	15	13	14	15											
FY05 plan (2004)					9	6	8	9	17	14	15	14	16	15										
FY06 plan (2005)						4	7	7	9	10	12	n/a	n/a	n/a	n/a									
FY07 plan (2006)							7	7	11	12	14	13	11	11	11	10								
FY08 plan (2007)								7	11	12	13	12	12	10	12	11	6							
FY09 plan (2008)									7	8	8	12	12	13	13	12	12	13						
FY10 plan (2009)										8	n/a	n/a	n/a	n/a	n/a	n/a	n/a	n/a	n/a					
FY11 plan (2010)											9	8	12	9	12	9	12	9	13	9				
FY12 plan (2011)												10	13	11	12	9	12	10	12	8	9			
FY13 plan (2012)													10	7	8	9	7	11	8	12	9	12		
FY14 plan (2013)														8	8	7	9	9	10	10	10	11	14	
FY15 plan (2014)															7	8	11	10	8	11	8	11	11	13

Source: Navy 30-year shipbuilding plans supplemented by annual Navy budget submissions (including 5-year shipbuilding plans) for fiscal years shown. **n/a** means not available—see notes below.

Notes: The FY2001 30-year plan submitted in 2000 was submitted under a one-time-only legislative provision, Section 1013 of the FY2000 National Defense Authorization Act (S. 1059/P.L. 106-65 of October 5, 1999). No provision required DOD to submit a 30-year shipbuilding plan in 2001 or 2002, when Congress considered DOD's proposed FY2002 and FY2003 DOD budgets. (In addition, no FYDP was submitted in 2001, the first year of the George W. Bush Administration.) Section 1022 of the FY2003 Bob Stump National Defense Authorization Act (H.R. 4546/P.L. 107-314 of December 2, 2002) created a requirement to submit a 30-year shipbuilding plan each year, in conjunction with each year's defense budget. This provision was codified at 10 U.S.C. 231. The first 30-year plan submitted under this provision was the one submitted in 2003, in conjunction with the proposed FY2004 DOD budget. For the next several years, 30-year shipbuilding plans were submitted each year, in conjunction with each year's proposed DOD budget. An exception occurred in 2009, the first year of the Obama Administration, when DOD submitted a proposed budget for FY2010 with no accompanying FYDP or 30-year Navy shipbuilding plan. Section 1023 of the FY2011 Ike Skelton National Defense Authorization Act (H.R. 6523/P.L. 111-383 of January 7, 2011) amended 10 U.S.C. 231 to require DOD to submit a 30-year shipbuilding plan once every four years, in the same year that DOD submits a Quadrennial Defense Review (QDR). Consistent with Section 1023, DOD did not submit a new 30-year shipbuilding plan at the time that it submitted the proposed FY2012 DOD budget. At the request of the House Armed Services Committee, the Navy submitted the FY2012 30-year (FY2012-FY2041) shipbuilding plan in late-May 2011. Section 1011 of the FY2012 National Defense Authorization Act (H.R. 1540/P.L. 112-81 of December 31, 2011) amended 10 U.S.C. 231 to reinstate the requirement to submit a 30-year shipbuilding plan each year, in conjunction with each year's defense budget.

Table 6. Projected Navy Force Sizes in First 10 years of 30-Year Shipbuilding Plans

Years shown are fiscal years; where two figures are shown, the first is the figure using existing rules for counting battle force ships, and the second is the figure using the Navy's proposed modified rules for counting battle force ships.

FY of 30-year plan (year submitted)	01	02	03	04	05	06	07	08	09	10	11	12	13	14	15	16	17	18	19	20	21	22	23	24
FY01 plan (2000)	316	315	313	313	313	311	311	304	305	305														
FY02 plan (2001)		316	n/a	n/a	n/a	n/a	n/a	n/a	n/a	n/a	n/a													
FY03 plan (2002)			314	n/a	n/a	n/a	n/a	n/a	n/a	n/a	n/a	n/a												
FY04 plan (2003)				292	292	291	296	301	305	308	313	317	321											
FY05 plan (2004)					290	290	298	303	308	307	314	320	328	326										
FY06 plan (2005)						289	293	297	301	301	306	n/a	n/a	305										
FY07 plan (2006)							285	294	299	301	306	315	317	315	314	317								
FY08 plan (2007)								286	289	293	302	310	311	307	311	314	322							
FY09 plan (2008)									286	287	289	290	293	287	288	291	301	309						
FY10 plan (2009)										287	n/a	n/a	n/a	n/a	n/a	n/a	n/a	n/a	n/a					
FY11 plan (2010)											284	287	287	285	285	292	298	305	311	315				
FY12 plan (2011)												290	287	286	286	297	301	311	316	322	324			
FY13 plan (2012)													285	279	276	284	285	292	300	295	296	298		
FY14 plan (2013)														282	270	280	283	291	300	295	296	297	297	
FY15 plan (2014)															274/ 284	280/ 290	286/ 296	295/ 304	301/ 309	304/ 308	304/ 307	306/ 307	311/ 314	313/ 315

Source: Navy 30-year shipbuilding plans supplemented by annual Navy budget submissions (including 5-year shipbuilding plans) for fiscal years shown. **n/a** means not available—see notes below.

Notes: The FY2001 30-year plan submitted in 2000 was submitted under a one-time-only legislative provision, Section 1013 of the FY2000 National Defense Authorization Act (S. 1059/P.L. 106-65 of October 5, 1999). No provision required DOD to submit a 30-year shipbuilding plan in 2001 or 2002, when Congress considered DOD's proposed FY2002 and FY2003 DOD budgets. Section 1022 of the FY2003 Bob Stump National Defense Authorization Act (H.R. 4546/P.L. 107-314 of December 2, 2002) created a requirement to submit a 30-year shipbuilding plan each year, in conjunction with each year's defense budget. This provision was codified at 10 U.S.C. 231. The first 30-year plan submitted under this provision was the one submitted in 2003, in conjunction with the proposed FY2004 DOD budget. For the next several years, 30-year shipbuilding plans were submitted each year, in conjunction with each year's proposed DOD budget. An exception occurred in 2009, the first year of the Obama Administration, when DOD submitted a proposed budget for FY2010 with no accompanying FYDP or 30-year Navy shipbuilding plan. The FY2006 plan included data for only selected years beyond FY2011. Section 1023 of the FY2011 Ike Skelton National Defense Authorization Act (H.R. 6523/P.L. 111-383 of January 7, 2011) amended 10 U.S.C. 231 to require DOD to submit a 30-year shipbuilding plan once every four years, in the same year that DOD submits a Quadrennial Defense Review (QDR). Consistent with Section 1023, DOD did not submit a new 30-year shipbuilding plan at the time that it submitted the proposed FY2012 DOD budget. At the request of the House Armed Services Committee, the Navy submitted the FY2012 30-year (FY2012-FY2041) shipbuilding plan in late-May 2011. Section 1011 of the FY2012 National Defense Authorization Act (H.R. 1540/P.L. 112-81 of December 31, 2011) amended 10 U.S.C. 231 to reinstate the requirement to submit a 30-year shipbuilding plan each year, in conjunction with each year's defense budget.

Oversight Issues for Congress for FY2015

Mid-Life Refueling Overhaul of Aircraft Carrier *George Washington* (CVN-73)

One potential oversight issue for Congress concerns the Navy's proposal to defer until FY2016 a decision on whether to proceed with the mid-life nuclear refueling overhaul of the aircraft carrier *George Washington* (CVN-73). To operate for a full 50-year life, existing Nimitz (CVN-68) class nuclear-powered carriers are given a mid-life nuclear refueling overhaul, called a refueling complex overhaul (RCOH), when they are 20 to 25 years old, which is when their original nuclear fuel core has been exhausted. The RCOH gives the ship a new nuclear fuel core sufficient to power the ship for the remainder of its 50-year life. The RCOH also involves a significant amount of other overhaul, repair, and modernization work on the ship. An RCOH requires about 44 months from contract award to delivery. RCOHs are funded through the Navy's shipbuilding account (the Shipbuilding and Conversion, Navy [SCN] appropriation account).

RCOHs are done primarily at Huntington Ingalls Industries/Newport News Shipbuilding (HII/NNS) in Newport News, VA, and form a significant part of HII/NNS's business base, along with construction of new nuclear-powered aircraft carriers and construction of new nuclear-powered submarines. RCOHs in recent years have been scheduled in a more or less heel-to-toe fashion at HII/NNS—when one RCOH is done, the next one is scheduled to begin soon thereafter. RCOHs are done in a particular dry dock at HII/NNS, so a carrier undergoing an RCOH in that dry dock must have its work finished and depart the dry dock before the following carrier can be moved into the dry dock for its RCOH.

The next carrier scheduled for an RCOH is the *George Washington* (CVN-73). The total estimated cost of the CVN-73 RCOH in the Navy's FY2014 budget submission was $4,738.2 million (i.e., about $4.7 billion).

Until the FY2015 budget submission, the CVN-73 RCOH was scheduled for FY2016. The CVN-73 RCOH received $12 million in advance procurement (AP) funding in FY2012, $69.9 million in AP funding in FY2013, and $245.8 million in AP funding in FY2014. Under the Navy's FY2014 budget submission, another $491.1 million in AP funding was projected for FY2015, and the balance of the RCOH's estimated cost of $4,738.2 million was to be provided in FY2016 and FY2017.

As part of its FY2015 budget submission, DOD removed funding for the CVN-73 RCOH from the FY2015-FY2019 Future Years Defense Plan (FYDP) and is proposing to defer the question of whether to proceed with the CVN-73 RCOH until next year, when Congress will consider the FY2016 defense budget. The Navy's proposed FY2015 budget includes about $46 million in funding in the Operation and Maintenance, Navy (OMN) appropriation account to defuel CVN-73. Defueling the ship (i.e., removing the original nuclear fuel core) is an initial step to be performed on the ship at NNS, regardless of whether the ship is to undergo an RCOH or be inactivated.

DOD and Navy officials state that if Congress provides an indication this year that it supports the defense spending levels in the FY2015-FY2019 FYDP, which are higher than those called for in the Budget Control Act of 2011 as amended, then the FYDP would be reformulated for FY2016 and subsequent years to include the roughly $7.0 billion in additional funding that would be needed over the FYDP to fund the CVN-73 RCOH and keep the ship and its associated carrier air wing in service.[6] Of this $7.0 billion in additional funding, $796.2 million would be required in FY2015.[7]

DOD and Navy officials state that if Congress does not provide an indication this year that it supports the defense spending levels in the FYDP, CVN-73 would instead be inactivated (i.e., permanently retired from service), and its associated air wing would be disestablished. Other things held equal, inactivating CVN-73 would reduce the Navy's carrier force to 10 ships for the next 25 years or so (i.e., the period of time that CVN-73 would have remained in service if it had received an RCOH).

The Navy states that, of the funding for the CVN-73 RCOH that was provided in FY2012 and FY2013, $20.6 million represent sunk costs that would not be recoverable if CVN-73 were not to receive an RCOH. The Navy states that this $20.6 million "primarily supported prime contractor and government initial planning efforts for the refueling overhaul as well as some initial modernization GFI [government-furnished information] development efforts."[8]

Navy officials state that deferring until next year the decision on whether to proceed with the CVN-73 RCOH would mean that the RCOH, if were to occur, would be delayed some number of months from the schedule shown in the Navy's FY2014 budget submission, and consequently would likely become an FY2017 action rather than an FY2016 action. Navy officials state that if the delay in the start of the RCOH were not more than a certain number of months, it would not cause a cascading delay in the schedule for the following RCOH (to be done on CVN-74), because there is currently some slack time on the back end of the CVN-73 RCOH period to absorb some delay in the CVN-73 RCOH without affecting the schedule for the CVN-74 RCOH.

10 U.S.C. 5062(b) states, "The naval combat forces of the Navy shall include not less than 11 operational aircraft carriers." The requirement as stated in this statute is not contingent on the DOD budget being at a certain level in coming years. To the contrary, the central purpose of 10 U.S.C. 5062(b) is to act as a mandate to the executive branch to support force of not less than 11 carriers in executive branch planning, regardless of budgetary or other circumstances. DOD has not, as part of its FY2015 budget submission, requested that 10 U.S.C. 5062(b) be amended or repealed.

Potential oversight questions for Congress include the following:

---

[6] The estimated total cost to perform the CVN-73 RCOH and retain the carrier and its associated air wing is about $8.1 billion. (This figure includes about $5.9 to perform the RCOH and keep the ship in service, about $1.4 billion to retain the air wing, and about $800 million for associated logistics, manpower, and training costs.) The FY2015-FY2019 FYDP currently includes about $1.1 billion to support the inactivation of CVN-73. Reprogramming this $1.1 billion in inactivation funding to support the RCOH would leave a requirement for about $7.0 billion in additional funding. Source: Navy information paper provided to CRS by Navy Office of Legislative Affairs on April 7, 2014.

[7] The total estimated requirement for FY2015 is $842.2 million. This figure includes the $46 million currently in the budget for the ship's defueling, leaving a net requirement of $796.2 million in additional funding for FY2015. Source: Navy information paper provided to CRS by Navy Office of Legislative Affairs on April 7, 2014.

[8] Source: Navy information paper dated March 13, 2014, and provided to CRS by the Navy Office of Legislative Affairs on April 17, 2014.

- Is DOD's proposal to treat the issue of whether to proceed with the CVN-73 RCOH (and consequently whether there are to be 10 or 11 carriers for the next 25 years or so) as a question to be decided next year, depending on indications of congressional support for a certain DOD budget level in coming years, consistent with 10 U.S.C. 5062(b)? Does DOD's proposal in effect treat the 11-carrier requirement in 10 U.S.C. 5062(b) as an optional matter rather than a mandate? If so, would this create a precedent for the executive branch to treat similar provisions in the U.S. Code as optional matters rather than mandates? For example, would it create a precedent for DOD, if it so desired, to begin treating as an optional matter the long-standing requirement in 10 U.S.C. 5063(a) that the Marine Corps "shall be so organized as to include not less than three combat divisions and three air wings, and such other land combat, aviation, and other services as may be organic therein?" If the executive branch were to begin treating statutory provisions like 10 U.S.C. 5062(b) as optional matters rather than mandates, what implications might this have for policy and program execution, and for Congress's power to legislatively establish policy and program goals?

- What would be the operational impact for the Navy of reducing the carrier force to 10 ships for the next 25 years or so (and also eliminating its associated carrier air wing)? What impact would it have on the Navy's ability to fulfill its missions?

- If the FDYP were reformulated to include the $7 billion in additional funding needed to keep CVN-73 and its associated air wing, what other defense programs would have their funding reduced, and what would be the impact of these reductions on DOD's ability to fulfill its missions?

- What would be the impact on HII/NNS and the other parts of the aircraft carrier industrial base if CVN-73 were inactivated rather than given an RCOH? What impact, if any, would this have on the cost of other work performed at NNS during these years, and on the eventual cost of the CVN-74 RCOH?[9]

Proposal to Put 11 Cruisers into Reduced Operating Status

A total of 27 Ticonderoga (CG-47) class Aegis cruisers (CGs 47 through 73) were procured for the Navy between FY1978 and FY1988; the ships entered service between 1983 and 1994. The first five ships in the class (CGs 47 through 51), which were built to an earlier technical standard in certain respects, were judged by the Navy to be too expensive to modernize and were removed from service in 2004-2005, leaving 22 ships in operation (CGs 52 through 73).

As a cost-saving measure, the Navy's FY2015 budget proposes putting the 11 youngest Aegis cruisers (CGs 63 through 73) into some form of reduced operating status starting in FY2015. While in reduced operating status, the ships would be modernized in preparation for their eventual return to full operational status. The ships would be returned to full operational status

---

[9] For press reports discussing the industrial-base aspects of the issue, see Lara Seligman, "Shipbuilder: Navy's Timeline For CVN-73 'Not In Accordance With Our Plan,'" *Inside the Navy*, March 24, 2014; Olga Belogolova, "PEO Carriers: A Cut From 11 To 10 Carriers Would Impact Industrial Base," *Inside the Navy*, February 24, 2014; Michael Fabey, "Foregoing Carrier RCOH Won't Disrupt Future Work, HII CEO Says," *Aerospace Daily & Defense Report*, March 25, 2014: 4; Rick Giannini and Darrell Grow, "Why Aircraft Carrier Workers Deserve a Better Plan from the Pentagon," *Defense One (www.defenseone.com)*, March 23, 2014.

years from now, as one-for-one replacements for the 11 older Aegis cruisers that are to remain in full operational status (CGs 52 through 62), as each of those 11 older cruisers reaches the end of its service life. Among the 11 Aegis cruisers that are proposed for reduced operating status are four that are capable of ballistic missile defense (BMD) operations.[10] Under a reported preliminary version of the Navy's plan, the 11 cruisers put into reduced operating status would return to service between FY2019 and FY2026, and the ships would operate into the 2030s and (in some cases) the 2040s.[11] Potential oversight questions for Congress include the following:

- What are the comparative costs to keep the 11 cruisers in operation vs. putting them into reduced operating status?

- What are the potential operational impacts of putting the 11 cruisers into reduced operating status? How would it affect the Navy's ability to perform its missions?

- The 11 cruisers have limited remaining growth potential. Will that growth potential be enough for the ships to support the combat system equipment that would be needed to keep the ships mission effective into the 2030s and 2040s?

- The CG-47s have crews of 300 or more personnel. By the 2030s and 2040s, the Navy will include some number of newer-design surface combatants that incorporate technologies for reducing crew size so as to reduce annual operating and support (O&S) costs. Assuming the 11 CG-47s could be made mission effective (see previous question), would they be considered mission cost effective, given their crew-related costs, by future Navy leaders compared to other Navy surface combatants in the 2030s and 2040s?

- In light of the two previous questions, can current Navy leaders guarantee that future Navy leaders years from now will follow-through on the plan to bring these 11 cruisers back into service and operate them into the 2030s and 2040s? If Navy leaders cannot guarantee this, how does that affect the balance of potential costs and benefits of the Navy's plan?

- Given that the 11 cruisers would be assigned minimal caretaker crews rather than full crews during the time they are in reduced operating status, how many of these 11 cruisers could be quickly returned to full operational status and deployed in response to a contingency that might require these ships? If the answer is less than 11, then should all 11 continue to be included in the count of battle force ships, as the Navy is doing in its FY2015 30-year shipbuilding plan?

A May 22, 2014, press report states:

> It would not be a "bad thing" if Congress ultimately blocks the Navy from taking half its cruisers out of service next year as long as lawmakers follow a historical pattern of providing the funds to keep the ships operating, Chief of Naval Operations Adm. Jonathan Greenert said Wednesday [May 21].

---

[10] These four ships are CG-67 (Shiloh), CG-70 (Lake Erie), CG-72 (Vella Gulf), and CG-73 (Port Royal). For more on the Aegis BMD program, see CRS Report RL33745, *Navy Aegis Ballistic Missile Defense (BMD) Program: Background and Issues for Congress*, by Ronald O'Rourke.

[11] See USNI News Editor, "Navy's New 'Battle Force' Tally To Include Hospital Ships and Small Patrol Craft," *USNI News* (http://news.usni.org), March 11, 2014.

Greenert told reporters the Navy's 2015 budget proposal that includes sidelining 11 of the 22 cruisers for long-term modernization was not an ideal solution but instead driven by spending constraints. If Congress can pay to operate the ships, the Navy will keep active, he said.

"It's not a good idea to put into a modernization availability a ship before it really needs to go in and that is not something we wanted to do but felt we were compelled to do," Greenert said at a breakfast hosted by the Defense Writers Group. "So if the decision is 'no, I don't want you do that, here's the money, continue to operate those ships,' that's not a bad thing."

"We need ships," he added....

"What would be optimal is that we continue to operate (the ships) and then when the time comes bring them in for modernization," he said. "But I need operating money to do that, personnel money, and we don't have that in the funds given to us."[12]

Proposal to Retire All 10 Remaining FFG-7 Frigates in FY2015

As another cost-saving measure, the Navy as part of its FY2015 budget submission is proposing to retire all 10 of its remaining Oliver Hazard Perry (FFG-7) class frigates in FY2015. By comparison, under the Navy's FY2014 budget submission, the Navy planned to retire seven of the ships in FY2015, two more in FY2017, and the final ship in FY2020. The proposed retirements of these frigates contribute to the projected shortfall in small surface combatants shown in the earlier years of **Table 4**. Potential oversight questions for Congress include the following:

- What are the comparative costs to keep some or all of these 10 frigates in service vs. retiring them in FY2015?

- What are the potential operational impacts of retiring all 10 of these frigates in FY2015? How would it affect the Navy's ability to perform its missions?

- Retired FFG-7 class frigates in some cases have been transferred to foreign navies. What are the Navy's plans regarding the post-retirement disposition of the 10 remaining FFG-7 frigates?

Proposal to Modify What Ships Are Included in the Count of Battle Force Ships

As mentioned earlier, the Navy as part of its FY2015 budget submission is proposing to modify the rules for what ships to include in the count of the total number of battle force ships in the Navy. The current counting rules date back to an agreement between the Navy and the Office of the Secretary of Defense in 1981. The Navy's proposed changes would:

- include certain ships in the count that have been routinely requested by a U.S. regional combatant commander (COCOM) and allocated among requesting COCOMs via DOD's Global Force Management Allocation Plan (GFMAP)—such ships would be included in the count on a case-by-case basis as

---

[12] Mike McCarthy, "'Not A Bad Thing' If Congress Blocks Attempt To Sideline Cruisers, Navy Chief Says," *Defense Daily*, May 22, 2014: 2-3.

recommended by the Chief of Naval Operations (CNO) with the approval of the Secretary of the Navy, as a temporary authorization that would remain in effect in the ships were no longer requested or were retired; and

- exclude ships from the count that are not self-deployable, unless they are forward deployed (i.e., forward homeported or forward stationed) and approved for inclusion in the count by the Secretary of the Navy.

The effect of these changes would be to include in the count the Navy's 10 Cyclone (PC-1) class patrol craft, which are currently operating in the Persian Gulf region, the Navy's two hospital ships (TAHs), and one high-speed transport (HST) ship, while excluding from the count three mine countermeasures (MCM) ships. As discussed earlier in connection with **Table 4**, these proposed changes would affect the reported figures for small surface combatants during the period FY2015-FY2024 and the reported figures for support ships during the period FY2015-FY2035.

In proposing the changes, the Navy argues that the current counting rules "do not capture special situations, such as regional demand [for ships], where non-battle force ships should be counted on a temporary basis." The Navy argues that the proposed new rules are "more flexible in response to Global Force Management Plans and COCOM demand signals."[13] They could also argue that the largest single proposed modification—the inclusion of the Navy's 10 Cyclone (PC-1) class patrol boats in the count—is consistent with the inclusion of certain patrol craft of the day (then designated PGs and PHMs) in the original 1981 definition of the types of ships to be counted as battle force ships.

Skeptics could argue that the proposed changes, if implemented, would make it harder to compare total numbers of battle force ships over time on an apples-to-apples basis, and that they would complicate congressional oversight by making the rules less transparent to outsiders, particularly in terms reconstructing or auditing figures for prior years, since doing so would require access to records of where individual ships were homeported in a given year and which Secretary of the Navy approvals were in effect in a given year. Skeptics might also argue that these changes are being proposed at a time that the Navy is proposing to remove ships from service as a cost-saving measure, and that the changes, if implemented, would have the effect of obscuring the resulting reduction in the size of the Navy.[14]

Potential Impact on Size of Navy of Limiting DOD Spending to BCA Caps Through FY2021

Another potential issue for Congress concerns the potential impact on the size of the Navy of limiting DOD spending through FY2021 to levels at or near the caps established in the Budget

---

[13] Source: Navy briefing charts on FY2015 30-year shipbuilding plan. See also letter from Secretary of the Navy Ray Mabus to The Honorable Richard J. Durbin, March 7, 2014, posted at USNI News (http news.usni.org), March 11, 2014.

[14] For press reports discussing the Navy's proposed changes in counting rules, see Christopher P. Cavas, "New Counting Rules Add Up To More Ships," *DefenseNews.com*, March 11, 2014; USNI News Editor, "Navy's New 'Battle Force' Tally to Include Hospital Ships and Small Patrol Craft," *USNI News* (http://news.usni.org), March 11, 2014; Sydney J. Freedberg, Jr., "Outrage On Capitol Hill As Navy Changes Ship-Counting Rules," *Breaking Defense* (http://breakingdefense.com), March 11, 2014.

Control Act of 2011 (BCA) as amended. Navy officials state that a decision to reduce DOD's budget to such levels would eventually lead to a smaller Navy.

Admiral Jonathan Greenert, the Chief of Naval Operations, provided detailed testimony on this question in his prepared statements for hearings before the Senate Armed Services Committee on November 7, 2013, and the House Armed Services Committee on September 18, 2013. In his prepared statement for the November 7, 2013, hearing, which was similar to his prepared statement for the September 18, 2013, hearing, Greenert testified that

> Consistent with what the Deputy Secretary of Defense told this committee in August, if fiscally constrained to the revised discretionary caps, over the long term (2013-2023), the Navy of 2020 would not be able to execute the missions described in the DSG [Defense Strategic Guidance]. There are numerous ways to adjust Navy's portfolio of programs to meet the BCA revised discretionary caps. These are currently under deliberation within the department. As requested, the following provides perspective on the level and type of adjustments that will need to be made.
>
> Any scenario to address the fiscal constraints under current law must include sufficient readiness, capability and manpower to complement the force structure capacity of ships and aircraft. This balance would need to be maintained to ensure each unit will be effective, even if the overall fleet is not able to execute the DSG. There are, however, many ways to balance between force structure, readiness, capability and manpower.
>
> One potential fiscal and programmatic scenario would result in a "2020 Fleet" of about 255-260 ships, about 30 less than today, and about 40 less than Navy's PB-14 [President's Budget for FY2014] submission. It would include 1-2 fewer CSG [carrier strike groups], and 1-2 fewer ARG [amphibious ready groups] than today. This 2020 fleet would not meet the DSG requirements for the mission to Provide a Stabilizing Presence. As a result, Navy would be less able to reinforce deterrence, build alliances and partnerships and influence events abroad.
>
> • Navy would not increase our global deployed presence, which would remain at about 95 ships in 2020. The lethality inherent in this presence, based on ship type deployed, would be less than today's 95-ship presence.
>
> • Navy would not increase presence in the Asia-Pacific, which would stay at about 50 ships in 2020. This would largely negate the ship force structure portion of our plan to rebalance to the Asia Pacific region directed by the DSG.
>
> • Navy would not "place a premium on U.S. military presence in—and in support of—partner nations" in the Middle East, since presence would decrease and, assuming we use the same ship deployment scheme in the future, there would be gaps in CSG presence totaling 2-3 months each year.
>
> • Navy would still "evolve our posture" in Europe by meeting our ballistic missile defense European Phased Adaptive Approach (EPAA) requirements with four BMD-capable DDG homeported in Rota, Spain and two land based sites in Romania and Poland. Additional presence would still be provided by forward operating JHSV, MLP, AFSB and some rotationally deployed combatants.
>
> • Navy would still provide "innovative, low-cost, and small-footprint approaches" to security in Africa and South America by deploying, on average, one JHSV and one LCS continuously to both regions and maintaining an AFSB in AFRICOM's area of responsibility.

In order to sustain a balance of force structure (current and future), modernization and personnel within our portfolio, continued compliance with the BCA revised discretionary caps would compel us to reduce our investments in force structure and modernization, which would result in a "2020 Fleet" that would not meet DSG direction in the following mission areas:

Counter Terrorism and Irregular Warfare (CT/IW). We would not have the capacity to conduct widely distributed CT/IW missions, as defined in the DSG. There would be inadequate LCS available to allocate to this non-core Navy mission, in the amount defined by the FSA and concurred upon by Special Operations Command.

Deter and Defeat Aggression. We would not be able to conduct one large-scale operation and also counter aggression by an opportunistic aggressor in a second theater. In this scenario, the fleet would have 9-10 CVN/CSG and 9-10 LHA/D and ARG. We would be able to sustain about one non-deployed CSG and one non-deployed ARG fully certified and able to surge on required timelines. Together, our presence and surge forces would be sufficient to conduct all missions associated with only one large scale operation, as defined today. This overall force and associated readiness would, however, be sufficient to execute Navy elements of the DSG mission to Conduct Stability and Counterinsurgency Operations.

Project Power Despite Anti-Access/Area Denial (A2/AD) Challenges. Overall, in this scenario, development of our capabilities to project power would not stay ahead of potential adversaries' A2/AD capabilities. We will not meet the projected capability requirements to assure Joint access in a plausible operational scenario in 2020 due to shortfalls, in particular, in air and missile defense:

• Some undersea capabilities will be slowed:

• Attainment of the required P-8A inventory (117) would be delayed from 2019 to 2020, and transition from the P-3C to the P-8A would be delayed from 2019 to 2020.

• Anti-submarine warfare combat system upgrades for DDGs and MFTA installations would not be affected.

• The LCS ASW Mission Package would be delayed from 2016 to 2017.

• Upgraded sonobuoys and advanced torpedo procurement would still equip all of our helicopters, SSN, and P-8A in the Western Pacific by 2018.

• Virginia Payload Module (VPM) would still be fielded in 2027 to enable Virginia-class SSN to replace SSGN that begin retiring in 2026.

• The LCS mine warfare mission package would still field its first increment in 2015 and the second in 2019.

• Air and missile defense improvements would be slowed:

• SEWIP upgraded electromagnetic sensing and upgraded jamming and deception capabilities would both be delayed one year (to 2015 and 2018, respectively). Both of these upgrades are required to counter advances in adversary anti-ship cruise missiles.

• The new Air and Missile Defense Radar (AMDR) would be delivered on only four ships, as compared to seven under our PB-14 submission, between 2021 and 2024.

• The Evolved Sea Sparrow Missile (ESSM) Block II would still be fielded in 2020, with 80 missiles being delivered to deployed ships.

• The F-35C Lightning II, the carrier-based variant of the Joint Strike Fighter, would still field in 2019 and join our CVW forward homeported in the Western Pacific in 2020. Overall, the number of F-35 procured would decrease by about 30 aircraft in 2020.

• All components of the improved air-to-air IR "kill chain" that circumvents adversary radar jamming would be delayed by two years. The Infrared Search and Track (IRST) sensor system would field in 2018 and the improved longer-range IRST would not deliver until 2021. The new longer-range AIM-9X Block III missile would not be fielded until 2023.

• Improvements to the air-to-air RF "kill chain" would be slowed down as F/A-18E/F Block II Super Hornet anti-jamming upgrades would be delayed to 2020. The longer-range AIM-120D missile would still field in 2014 but equipping of all Pacific carrier air wings would be delayed by two years to 2022.

• The Navy Integrated Fire Control – Counter Air (NIFC-CA) network would still initially field with the E-2D Advanced Hawkeye in 2015, but only four CVW (compared to six in our PB-14 submission) would have it by 2020. Transition to the E-2D would be delayed three years to 2025.

Operate Effectively in Space and Cyber Space. Plans to recruit, hire and train 976 additional cyber operators and form 40 computer operations teams by 2017 would not be impacted. This is a priority in any fiscal scenario. However, the BCA's reduced funding levels would delay replacement of our cyber systems and decrease our ability to defend our networks.

Maintain a Safe, Secure, and Effective Nuclear Deterrent. We would still be able to sustain today's ballistic missile submarine (SSBN) force. The SSBN(X) would still deliver in 2030 to replace retiring Ohio class SSBN while meeting requirements for SSBN presence and surge. This is the top priority program for the Navy.

Defend the Homeland and Provide Support to Civil Authorities. We would still meet the capacity requirements for these missions.

Counter Weapons of Mass Destruction. We would still meet the presence requirements for this mission.

Conduct Humanitarian, Disaster Relief, and Other Operations. We would still meet the presence requirements for this mission.

The extent of the fiscal changes in the BCA, when compared to current program and budget levels, would compel Navy to request relief from several program mandates and force structure capacity limits, in order to sustain and build a fleet with a balance of ship types. For example, mandated limits govern the size of the force, minimum funding for certain activities and facilities, and changes to the number of personnel at a base.[15]

---

[15] Statement of Admiral Jonathan Greenert, U.S. Navy, Chief of Naval Operations, Before the Senate Armed Services Committee on the Impact of Sequestration on the National Defense, November 7, 2013, pp. 7-11. For Greenert's statement for the September 18, 2013, hearing, see Statement of Admiral Jonathan Greenert, U.S. Navy, Chief of Naval Operations, Before the House Armed Services Committee on Planning for Sequestration in FY 2014 and Perspectives of the Military Services on the Strategic Choices and Management Review, September 18, 2013, pp. 6-10.

Appropriate Future Size and Structure of Navy in Light of Strategic and Budgetary Changes

Another potential oversight issue for Congress concerns the appropriate future size and structure of the Navy. Changes in strategic and budgetary circumstances have led to a broad debate over the future size and structure of the military, including the Navy. Changes in strategic circumstances include, among other things, the end of U.S. combat operations in Iraq, the winding down of U.S. combat operations in Afghanistan, China's military (including naval) modernization effort,[16] maritime territorial disputes involving China,[17] and Russia's actions to gain control of Crimea.

On January 5, 2012, the Administration announced that, in light of the end of U.S. combat operations in Iraq, the winding down of such operations in Afghanistan, and developments in the Asia-Pacific region, U.S. defense strategy in coming years will include a stronger focus on the Asia-Pacific region.[18] Since the Asia-Pacific region is primarily a maritime and aerospace theater for the DOD, this shift in strategic focus is expected by many observers to result in a shift in the allocation of DOD resources toward the Navy and Air Force. DOD officials have indicated that efforts to support a stronger focus on the Asia-Pacific region will be protected if planned levels of DOD spending in future years are reduced as a result of the BCA or other legislative action.

The Navy's current goal for a fleet of 306 ships reflects a number of judgments and planning factors (some of which the Navy receives from the Office of the Secretary of Defense), including but not limited to the following:

- U.S. interests and the U.S. role in the world, and the U.S. military strategy for supporting those interests and that role;

- current and projected Navy missions in support of U.S. military strategy, including both wartime operations and day-to-day forward-deployed operations;

- current and projected capabilities of potential adversaries, including their anti-access/area-denial (A2/AD) capabilities;

- regional combatant commander (COCOM) requests for forward-deployed Navy forces;

- the individual and networked capabilities of current and future Navy ships and aircraft;

- basing arrangements for Navy ships, including numbers and locations of ships homeported in foreign countries;

---

[16] For more on the modernization of China's military (particularly naval) capabilities and its potential implications for required U.S. Navy capabilities, see CRS Report RL33153, *China Naval Modernization: Implications for U.S. Navy Capabilities—Background and Issues for Congress*, by Ronald O'Rourke.

[17] For a discussion of these disputes, see CRS Report R42784, *Maritime Territorial and Exclusive Economic Zone (EEZ) Disputes Involving China: Issues for Congress*, by Ronald O'Rourke. See also CRS Report R42930, *Maritime Territorial Disputes in East Asia: Issues for Congress*, by Ben Dolven, Mark E. Manyin, and Shirley A. Kan.

[18] Department of Defense, *Sustaining U.S. Global Leadership: Priorities for 21st Century Defense*, January 2012, 8 pp. For more on this document, see CRS Report R42146, *Assessing the January 2012 Defense Strategic Guidance (DSG): In Brief*, by Catherine Dale and Pat Towell. See also CRS Report R42448, *Pivot to the Pacific? The Obama Administration's "Rebalancing" Toward Asia*, coordinated by Mark E. Manyin.

- maintenance and deployment cycles for Navy ships; and
- fiscal constraints.

With regard to the fourth point above, Navy officials testified in March 2014 that a Navy of 450 ships would be required to fully meet COCOM requests for forward-deployed Navy forces.[19] The difference between a fleet of 450 ships and the current goal for a fleet of 306 ships can be viewed as one measure of the operational risk associated with the goal of a fleet of 306 ships. A goal for a fleet of 450 ships might be viewed as a fiscally unconstrained goal.

Some study groups have made their own proposals for Navy ship force structure that reflect their own perspectives on the points listed above (particularly the first three and the final one) shows some of these proposals. For purposes of comparison, also shows the Navy's 306-ship goal of January 2013.

---

[19] Spoken testimony of Admiral Jonathan Greenert at a March 12, 2014, hearing before the House Armed Services Committee on the Department of the Navy's proposed FY2015 budget, as shown in transcript of hearing.

Table 7. Recent Study Group Proposals for Navy Ship Force Structure

Ship type	Navy's 306-ship goal of January 2013	Project on Defense Alternatives (PDA) (November 2012)	Heritage Foundation (April 2011)	Cato Institute (September 2010)[a]	Independent Panel Assessment of 2010 QDR (July 2010)	Sustainable Defense Task Force (June 2010)	Center for a New American Security (CNAS) (November 2008)	Center for Strategic and Budgetary Assessment (CSBA) (2008)[b]
Submarines								
SSBN	12	7	14[c]	6	14	7	14	12
SSGN	0	6-7	4	0	4	4	0	2
SSN	48	42	55	40	55	37	40	41
Aircraft carriers								
CVN	11	9	11	8	11	9	8	11
CVE	0	0	0	0	0	0	0	4
Surface combatants								
Cruiser	88	72-74	88	22	n/a	85	18	14
Destroyer				65	n/a		56	73
Frigate	0	2-7[i]	28[d]	14	n/a	0	0	9[e]
LCS	52	12[j]		4	n/a	25	48	55
SSC	0	[i]	0	0	n/a	0	40	0[f]
Amphibious and Maritime Prepositioning Force (Future) (MPF[F]) ships								
Amphibious ships	33	≥23	37	23	n/a	27	36	33
MPF(F) ships	0	n/a	0	0	n/a	n/a	0	3[g]
LSD station ships	0	0	0	0	0	0	0	7[h]
Other: Mine warfare (MIW) ships; Combat Logistics Force (CLF) ships (i.e., at-sea resupply ships), and support ships								
MIW	0	14[j]	14	11	0	0	0	0
CLF ships	29	n/a	33	21	n/a	36	40	31
Support ships	33	n/a	25	27	n/a			31
TOTAL battle force ships	306	230	309	241	346	230	300	326[j]

Source: Table prepared by CRS based on the following sources: **For Heritage Foundation:** *A Strong National Defense[:] The Armed Forces America Needs and What They Will Cost,* Heritage Foundation, April 5, 2011, pp. 25-26. **For Cato Institute:** Benjamin H. Friedman and Christopher Preble, *Budgetary Savings from Military Restraint,* Washington, Cato Institute, September 23, 2010 (Policy Analysis No. 667), pp. 6, 8-10, and additional information provided by Cato Institute to CRS by email on September 22, 2010. **For Independent Panel Assessment:** Stephen J. Hadley and William J. Perry, co-chairmen, et al., *The QDR in Perspective: Meeting America's National Security Needs In the 21st Century, The Final Report of the Quadrennial Defense Review Independent Panel,* Washington, 2010, Figure 3-2 on pages 58-59. **For Sustainable Defense Task Force:** *Debt, Deficits, and Defense, A Way Forward[:] Report of the Sustainable Defense Task Force,* June 11, 2010, pp. 19-20. **For CNAS:** Frank Hoffman, *From Preponderance to Partnership: American Maritime Power in the 21st Century.* Washington, Center for a New American Security, November 2008. p. 19 (Table 2). **For CSBA:** Robert O. Work, *The US Navy[:] Charting a Course for Tomorrow's Fleet.* Washington, Center for Strategic and Budgetary Assessments, 2008. p. 81 (Figure 5). **For PDA:** Carl Conetta, Reasonable Defense, Project on Defense Alternatives, November 14, 2012, 31 pp.

Notes: n/a is not addressed in the report. **SSBN** is nuclear-powered ballistic missile submarine; **SSGN** is nuclear-powered cruise missile and special operations forces submarine; **SSN** is nuclear-powered attack submarine; **CVN** is large nuclear-powered aircraft carrier; **CVE** is medium-sized aircraft carrier; **LCS** is Littoral Combat Ship; **SSC** (an acronym created by CRS for this table) is small surface combatant of 1,000+ tons displacement—a ship similar to late-1990s Streetfighter concept; **MPF(F)** is Maritime Prepositioning Force (Future) ship; **LSD** is LSD-41/49 class amphibious ship operating as a station ship for a formation like a Global Fleet Station (GFS); **MIW** is mine warfare ship; **CLF** is combat logistics force (i.e., resupply) ship.

a. Figures shown are for the year 2020; for subsequent years, reductions from these figures would be considered.

b. Figures shown are for the year 2028.

c. The report calls for a force of 280 SLBMs, which appears to equate to a force of 14 SSBNs, each with 20 SLBM tubes.

d. The report calls for a force of 28 small surface combatants, and appears to use the term small surface combatants the same way that the Navy does in the 30-year shipbuilding plan—as a way of collectively referring to frigates and LCSs. The small surface combatants (SSCs) called for in the November 2008 CNAS report are separate from and smaller than the LCS.

e. Maritime Security Frigates.

f. Plan includes 28 patrol craft (PCs) of a few hundred tons displacement each, as well as 29 boat detachments and seven riverine squadrons.

g. Plan shows three Mobile Landing Platform (MLP) ships that the Navy currently plans for the MPF(F) squadron, plus 16 existing current-generation maritime prepositioning force (MPF) ships and 17 existing prepositioning ships for Army and other service/agency equipment. Plan also shows 67 other DOD sealift ships.

h. T-LSDs, meaning LSDs operated by the Military Sealift Command (MSC) with a partly civilian crew.

i. The CSBA report shows a total of 488 units by including 162 additional force units that do not count toward the 306-ship goal under the battle force ships counting method that has been used since the early 1980s for public policy discussions of the size of the Navy. These 162 additional force units include 16 existing current-generation maritime prepositioning force (MPF) ships and 17 existing prepositioning ships for Army and other service/agency equipment, 67 other DOD sealift ships, 28 PCs, 29 boat detachments, and certain other small-scale units. The CSBA report proposes a new counting method for naval/maritime forces that includes units such as these in the total count.

j. The report "prescribes ending procurement of the LCS with the 12 already purchased. The *Reasonable Defense* model foresees a future cohort of 28 to 33 small surface combatants, including a mix of the 12 LCS that have already been procured, 14 Mine Counter Measure (MCM) ships already in the fleet, and small frigates or ocean-going corvettes. As the MCM ships age and leave the fleet, the LCS should assume their role. The would leave a post-MCM requirement for 16 to 21 additional small surface combatants. For this, the Navy needs a simpler, less expensive alternative to the LCS."

A potential key question for Congress concerns whether the U.S. Navy in coming years will be large enough to adequately counter improved Chinese maritime A2/AD forces while also adequately performing other missions of interest to U.S. policy makers around the world. Some observers are concerned that a combination of growing Chinese naval capabilities and budget-driven reductions in the size of the U.S. Navy could encourage Chinese military overconfidence and demoralize U.S. allies and partners in the Pacific, and thereby make it harder for the United States to defend its interests in the region.[20] Potential oversight questions for Congress include the following:

---

[20] See, for example, Dan Blumenthal and Michael Mazza, "Asia Needs a Larger U.S. Defense Budget," *Wall Street Journal*, July 5, 2011; J. Randy Forbes, "Defence Cuts Imperil US Asia Role," *The Diplomat* (http://the-diplomat.com), October 26, 2011. See also Andrew Krepinevich, "Panetta's Challenge," *Washington Post*, July 15, 2011: 15; Dean Cheng, *Sea Power and the Chinese State: China's Maritime Ambitions*, Heritage Foundation Backgrounder No. 2576, (continued...)

- Under the Administration's plans, will the Navy in coming years be large enough to adequately counter improved Chinese maritime A2/AD forces while also adequately performing other missions of interest to U.S. policy makers around the world?

- What might be the political and security implications in the Asia-Pacific region of a combination of growing Chinese naval capabilities and budget-driven reductions in the size of the U.S. Navy?

- If the Navy is reduced in size and priority is given to maintaining Navy forces in the Pacific, what will be the impact on Navy force levels in other parts of the world, such as the Persian Gulf/Indian Ocean region or the Mediterranean Sea, and consequently on the Navy's ability to adequately perform its missions in those parts of the world?

- To what extent could the operational impacts of a reduction in Navy ship numbers be mitigated through increased use of forward homeporting, multiple crewing, and long-duration deployments with crew rotation (i.e., "Sea Swap")? How feasible are these options, and what would be their potential costs and benefits?[21]

- Particularly in a situation of constrained DOD resources, if enough funding is allocated to the Navy to permit the Navy in coming years to maintain a fleet of 306 ships including 11 aircraft carriers, how much would other DOD programs need to be reduced, and what would be the operational implications of those program reductions in terms of DOD's overall ability to counter improved Chinese military forces and perform other missions?[22]

One observer—the person who has been the Navy's lead force-structure planner—stated the following regarding the Navy's approach to fleet design:

> It is time to rethink how we will design the future Fleet in a way that rebalances affordability, platform capability, and deployment processes. We must build it as a whole instead of continuing to "let it happen" one platform requirements decision at a time....
>
> Today the Navy operates about 50 different types of ships and aircraft with individual design-service lives of 20 to 50 years. On average, about two classes of ship or aircraft annually come up for a decision on replacement at the end of their service lives. Each of these decisions, a multi-year joint bureaucratic process with dozens of participating organizations, is made individually. Typically, as a starting point, the new platform must do everything the old one did, except in the more challenging threat environment of the future. All of the decision-making organizations generally advocate for the next-generation platform to have the desired capabilities unmet by the old one—particularly since any additional unit cost is not their bill. It is no surprise that this process leads to steadily increasing platform and overall Fleet cost....

(...continued)

July 11, 2011, p. 10.

[21] For further discussion of these options, see CRS Report RS21338, *Navy Ship Deployments: New Approaches—Background and Issues for Congress*, by Ronald O'Rourke.

[22] For further discussion, see CRS Report RL33153, *China Naval Modernization: Implications for U.S. Navy Capabilities—Background and Issues for Congress*, by Ronald O'Rourke.

The future Fleet is being designed ad hoc, one platform at a time, and we cannot afford this. How can we change the trend toward an ever-smaller Fleet of ever-better platforms while maintaining the capability superiority needed to execute our missions? It will take a top-down design to provide a structure in which individual platform requirements can be shaped and disciplined despite all of the pressures. We will have to consider distributing capabilities to a greater extent across a force that is securely networked, at least within line of sight, rather than putting as many as possible on each individual platform and continuing to drive up its size and cost.

We will have to consider separating weapon magazines from the sensors that direct the weapons rather than putting both on the same platform. Another option is increasing reliance on deep-magazine directed energy systems, and on force-wide coordinated soft-kill and counter-targeting techniques, rather than on engaging each threat with ever-larger and more expensive kinetic weapons. We can also think about increasing reliance on penetrating high-threat areas with longer-range weapons or with preprogrammed unmanned systems rather than with manned platforms. Few of these options would rise to the top in the requirements decision-making process for any individual platform. They only start to make sense when considered and competed at a Fleet-wide level.

Developing an overall fleet design to structure and discipline individual platform requirements is no small task. Simply constraining platform cost without dealing with how capabilities might be delivered differently is not sufficient. This is not a once-and-done process, as changes in threat and in our own technology options will never stop. But neither can it be a process that changes the design in some fundamental way every year or two—it will have to influence platform requirements for a long period of time to affect a significant number of new platform designs.

We cannot afford to retire legacy platforms prematurely simply because they are not optimized within our new Fleet design, which will take time to implement and have to be done incrementally. Real and fundamental change in the roles, missions, and interdependencies among platform types, and in the balance between manned and unmanned and between platform and payload, is an inevitable outcome of a Fleet design process. That is the point. Change is hard, and it will have to be authorized and directed by the Navy's leadership or risk not happening.

A number of ideas for a new Fleet design have been offered recently from outside the Navy's decision-making mainstream. However, all have had significant flaws, so they have not received serious consideration. They have assumed things such as beyond line-of-sight networking that has no survivable future in the face of adversary counter-space capability; autonomy of unmanned vehicles in executing lethal missions that is beyond the projected capability of software and U.S. rules of engagement to support; and the use of platforms too small to be capable of global deployment and sustained sea-based operations, which is how the U.S. Navy must deliver global naval power. The future Fleet design must be grounded in technical and operational reality, and it has to come from inside the Navy system....

Developing a rich list of operationally-realistic options supported by rigorous analysis of cost and feasibility is foundational. It could include:

• The use of a common large aviation-ship hull for Navy sea-control/power-projection air wings and for Marine Corps vertical-raid/assault-air wings, reconfigurable between the two missions between the deployments;

• Surface combatants with smaller vertical-launch magazines that can reload at sea from logistic ships or remotely fire weapons carried in supplementary magazines on logistic ships;

• Separate classes of surface combatants optimized for air defense or antisubmarine warfare within a common hull type that can self-defend in peacetime but aggregate to fight offensively in wartime;

• Tactical-combat aircraft that are optimized for endurance and carriage of long-range weapons rather than for penetrating sophisticated defenses carrying short-range weapons;

• Large shore-launched unmanned undersea vehicles that take the place of submarines for preprogrammed missions such as covert surveillance or mine-laying;

• Use of a common hull type for all of the large non-combatant ship missions such as command ships, tenders, hospital ships, ground vehicle delivery, and logistics; and

• Elimination of support models that are based on wartime reliance on reach-back access to unclassified cyber networks connected by vulnerable communications satellites or to an indefensible global internet....

The Navy's long-term force structure requirement is a 306-ship Fleet of the currently-planned designs, of which about 120 (or 40 percent of the force) would be deployed day-to-day. It would also be able to surge an additional 75 ships (another 25 percent) within two months to meet warfighting capacity requirements. In other words, about 65 percent is employed or rapidly employable.

This sounds good, but the reality is that 30 of these 120 deployed ships would be permanently homeported overseas; 26 would be LCSs that use the rotation of their small military crews to keep 50 percent of that class forward deployed; and 40 would be Military Sealift Command support ships that use rotational civilian mariner crewing to keep the ships deployed 75 percent of the time. The remaining 25 of the forward-deployed force will be large and complex multibillion dollar warships with all-military crews, supported out of a rotation base of 140 such ships.

In other words, we plan to buy and operate five of our most expensive ships to keep one deployed. This is not an efficient way to operate. In times of reduced funding our design must address ways to meet our deployment goals with a smaller rotation base while preserving wartime surge capacity.

Many studies and trials have been done over the years on options for reducing the total number of ships needed to sustain the Navy's robust peacetime forward-deployed posture. Increasing forward homeporting in other nations always comes up as the first choice. While it is a good one, few countries beyond those that currently support this (Japan, Spain, Italy, and Bahrain) are willing to tolerate a permanent new U.S. shore footprint. Building new shore-support infrastructure in foreign countries to back this results in a large bill for construction jobs outside the United States, which Congress normally finds unappetizing.

Using rotational crews to keep ships forward for extended periods without long deployments for their sailors is an efficient option that works for ships with small crews like LCSs, legacy mine-warfare ships, or Military Sealift Command support ships. Experiments in which this has been done with military crews on large complex warships have not turned out well. This was due both to the logistics of moving large crews overseas for turnovers and the difficulty of maintaining exact configuration commonality within ships of a class so that a crew arriving on a ship overseas has trained before deployment on an identical ship (or simulator) at home. Conversions of ships from military manning to Military Sealift Command civilian mariner crews that routinely rotate individual crewmembers to sustain ships forward are limited by the law of war concerning what military actions civilians can perform, and there are few legal options left for further expansion of this approach.

What is left in the force-generation model of our current Fleet is a force of our most complex warships—aircraft carriers, submarines, destroyers, and amphibious ships—operating with permanently-assigned military crews in the "Fleet Readiness Program" cycle of maintain-train-deploy with a deployed output of one in five. Future designs must address this model and find ways to get more deployed time out of these expensive ships and crews—without exceeding the current objective of having military crewmembers spend no more than 50 percent of their time away from homeport over a complete multi-year operating cycle. The current limiting factor is the period required to train the crew as a team before deployment following the inactivity and crew turnover of the shipyard maintenance period.

Naval aviation is steadily moving toward the increased use of high-fidelity single and multi-aircraft simulation as a means of developing and sustaining operational proficiency with reduced use of expensive live flying. These simulators are funded as part of the overall fielding plan for the aircraft and were also built for the ballistic-missile submarine force to support its Blue-Gold crew manning concept. There is no equivalent model or set of off-ship simulators for major sections of the crews of conventional surface warships (other than the LCS) for nuclear-aircraft carriers or for attack submarines. A Fleet design that bought such simulation capability as part of its ship production programs—the way that aircraft programs do—would have significant potential for improving operational output by reducing the time to train for deployment after maintenance periods.

Today's Fleet design is the product of many separate and disconnected decisions about the required capabilities of 50 different types of ships and aircraft. While not ineffective, it is definitely too expensive. The budget constraints facing the Navy for the next 20 years are not matched by a projected reduction in the quantity or capability of forces that must be delivered forward every day or surged forward in wartime.

The only way to meet these demands within available resources is to develop a design that provides a structure within which the capabilities of future platforms can be shaped to meet the Fleet's missions efficiently as an overall force. Doing this will require a systems-level approach to defining what it must be able to do, and will mean abandoning some cherished traditions of what each type of platform should do. The alternative is a Navy no longer large or capable enough to do the nation's business.[23]

Affordability of 30-Year Shipbuilding Plan

Another potential oversight issue for Congress concerns the prospective affordability of the Navy's 30-year shipbuilding plan. In assessing the prospective affordability of the 30-year plan, key factors that Congress may consider include estimated ship procurement costs and future shipbuilding funding levels.

Estimated Ship Procurement Costs

As mentioned earlier, the Navy's 30-year shipbuilding plan is based on certain assumptions, including assumptions about ship procurement costs. If one or more Navy ship designs turn out to be more expensive to build than the Navy estimates, then the projected funding levels shown in the 30-year shipbuilding plan will not be sufficient to procure all the ships shown in the plan. Ship designs that can be viewed as posing a risk of being more expensive to build than the Navy estimates include Gerald R. Ford (CVN-78) class aircraft carriers, Ohio-replacement (SSBNX)

---

[23] Arthur H. Barber, "Rethinking The Future Fleet," *U.S. Naval Institute Proceedings*, May 2014: 48-52.

class ballistic missile submarines, the Flight III version of the DDG-51 destroyer, the TAO(X) oiler, and the LX(R) amphibious ship.

In recent years, the Congressional Budget Office (CBO) has estimated that certain Navy ships would be more expensive to procure than the Navy estimates, and consequently that the Navy's 30-year shipbuilding plan would cost more to implement than the Navy has estimated. In its October 2013 report on the cost of the FY2014 30-year shipbuilding plan, the CBO estimates that the plan would cost an average of $19.3 billion per year in constant FY2013 dollars to implement, or about 15% more than the Navy estimates. CBO's estimate is about 6% higher than the Navy's estimate for the first 10 years of the plan, about 14% higher than the Navy's estimate for the second 10 years of the plan, and about 26% higher than the Navy's estimate for the final 10 years of the plan.[24] Some of the difference between CBO's estimate and the Navy's estimate, particularly in the latter years of the plan, is due to a difference between CBO and the Navy in how to treat inflation in Navy shipbuilding. **Table 8** summarizes the Navy and CBO estimates of the FY2014 30-year shipbuilding plans.

Table 8. Navy and CBO Estimates of Cost of FY2014 30-Year (FY2014-FY2043) Shipbuilding Plans

Funding for new-construction ships, in billions of constant FY2013 dollars

	First 10 years (FY2014-FY2023)	Next 10 years (FY2024-FY2033)	Final 10 years (FY2034-FY2043)	Entire 30 years (FY2014-FY2043)
Navy estimate	15.4	19.8	15.2	16.8
CBO estimate	16.3	22.6	19.1	19.3
% difference between Navy and CBO estimates	6%	14%	26%	15%

Source: Congressional Budget Office, *An Analysis of the Navy's Fiscal Year 2014 Shipbuilding Plan*, October 2013, Table 3 (page 13).

Future Shipbuilding Funding Levels

As mentioned earlier, the Navy's 30-year shipbuilding plan is based on certain assumptions, including assumptions about future shipbuilding funding levels. It has been known for some time that funding requirements for the Ohio-replacement (SSBN[X]) ballistic missile submarine program will put considerable pressure on the shipbuilding budget during the middle years of the 30-year plan. Although the FY2014 30-year shipbuilding plan reduces procurement of other types of ships in the middle years of the plan to help accommodate the SSBN(X) program, the Navy still projects that the shipbuilding budget would need to be substantially higher during the middle years of the plan than during the earlier or later years of the plan.

If the "hump" in shipbuilding funding during the middle years of the 30-year plan is not achieved, numerous ships shown for procurement during the middle years of the plan might not be procured. A potential oversight question for Congress is whether the Navy has received a commitment or assurance of some kind from DOD leaders that the Navy will be able to budget

---

[24] Congressional Budget Office, *An Analysis of the Navy's Fiscal Year 2014 Shipbuilding Plan*, October 2013, Table 3 (page 13).

for the "hump" in shipbuilding funding during the middle years of the 30-year plan without reducing funding for other Navy program priorities. The Navy's report on the FY2014 30-year shipbuilding plan states:

> The Department [of the Navy] will encounter several challenges in executing this shipbuilding plan; perhaps the most important is funding and delivering the *Ohio*-replacement (OR) program SSBN. The OR SSBN is projected to cost about $6 billion each [in constant FY2013 dollars]. Therefore, during the procurement and construction of OR SSBN between FY2021 and FY2035 an average of $19.2 billion per year is projected to be required for shipbuilding, which will be a key resourcing challenge for the Department.
>
> In addition to the challenge of funding the OR SSBN, during several years in the early 20202 [the] Navy will also require approximately $2 billion [per year] in additional ship construction funding to recapitalize the large number of ships decommissioning in those years. Our current fleet has a large cohort of ships that are about the same age and will thus retire as a group. These ships were built in the 1980s, some at a rate of three or four ships per year per class. These retiring ships will need to be recapitalized to reach the FSA-required battle force size and shape [i.e., the 306-ship goal]....
>
> DoN has historically been able to resource between $12B [billion] and $14B in annual new-ship procurement funding. During the FY2014-FY2018 FYDP, average annual new-ship procurement funding is about $14B. This level of investment is based on the need to balance our resources between manning, maintenance, sustainment, modernization and recapitalization of our ships, aircraft and weapons.
>
> The cost of the OR SSBN is significant relative to the resources available to DoN in any given year. At the same time, the Department will have to address the block retirement of ships procured in large numbers during the 1980s which are reaching the end of their service lives. The confluence of these events prevents DoN from being able to shift resources within the shipbuilding account to accommodate the cost of the OR SSBN.
>
> If DoN funds the OR SSBN from within its own resources, OR SSBN construction will take away from construction of other ships in the battle force such as attack submarines, destroyers, aircraft carriers and amphibious warfare shps. The resulting battle force will not meet the requirements of the FSA and will therefore not be sufficient to implement the DSG [Defense Strategic Guidance]. In addition there will be significant impact to the shipbuilding industrial base.[25]

In a situation of reduced levels of defense spending, such as what would occur if defense spending were to remain constrained to the revised cap levels in the Budget Control Act, the affordability challenge posed by the 30-year shipbuilding plan would be intensified. Even then, however, the current 30-year shipbuilding plan would not necessarily become unaffordable.[26]

The Navy estimates that, in constant FY2013 dollars, fully implementing the current 30-year shipbuilding plan would require an average of $16.8 billion in annual funding for new-construction ships, compared to a historic average of $12 billion to $14 billion provided for this

---

[25] *Report to Congress on the Annual Long-Range Plan for Construction of Naval Vessels for FY2014*, May 2013, pp. 11-12, 18-19.

[26] This paragraph and those that follow are adapted from Statement of Ronald O'Rourke, Specialist in Naval Affairs, Congressional Research Service, Before the House Armed Services Committee Subcommittee on Seapower and Projection Forces, on the Navy's FY2014 30-Year Shipbuilding Plan, October 23, 2013, pp. 1-4.

purpose.[27] The required increase in average annual funding of $2.8 billion to $4.8 billion per year equates to less than 1% of DOD's annual budget under the revised caps of the Budget Control Act. CBO estimates that, in constant FY2013 dollars, fully implementing the current 30-year shipbuilding plan would require an average of $19.3 billion in annual funding for new-construction ships, or $2.5 billion per year more than the Navy estimates.[28] This would make the required increase in average annual funding $5.3 billion to $7.3 billion per year, which equates to roughly 1.1% to 1.5% of DOD's annual budget under the revised caps of the Budget Control Act.

Some observers, noting the U.S. strategic rebalancing toward the Asia-Pacific region, have advocated shifting a greater share of the DOD budget to the Navy and Air Force, on the grounds that the Asia-Pacific region is primarily a maritime and aerospace theater for DOD. In discussing the idea of shifting a greater share of the DOD budget to the Navy and Air Force, some of these observers refer to breaking the so-called "one-third, one-third, one-third" division of resources among the three military departments—a shorthand term sometimes used to refer to the more-or-less stable division of resources between the three military departments that existed for the three decades between the end of U.S. participation in the Vietnam War in 1973 and the start of the Iraq War in 2003.[29] In a context of breaking the "one-third, one-third, one-third" allocation with an aim of better aligning defense spending with the strategic rebalancing, shifting 1.5% or less of DOD's budget into the Navy's shipbuilding account would appear to be quite feasible.

More broadly, if defense spending were to remain constrained to the revised cap levels in the Budget Control Act, then fully funding the Department of the Navy's total budget at the levels shown in the current Future Years Defense Plan (FYDP) would require increasing the Department of the Navy's share of the non-Defense-Wide part of the DOD budget to about 41%, compared to about 36% in the FY2014 budget and an average of about 37% for the three-decade period between the Vietnam and Iraq wars.[30] While shifting 4% or 5% of DOD's budget to the Department of the Navy would be a more ambitious reallocation than shifting 1.5% or less of the DOD budget to the Navy's shipbuilding account, similarly large reallocations have occurred in the past:

- From the mid-1950s to the mid-1960s, reflecting a U.S. defense strategy at the time that placed a strong reliance on the deterrent value of nuclear weapons, the

---

[27] See *Report to Congress on the Annual Long-Range Plan for Construction of Naval Vessels for FY2014*, May 2013, p. 18.

[28] Congressional Budget Office, *An Analysis of the Navy's Fiscal Year 2014 Shipbuilding Plan*, October 2013, Table 3 (page 13).

[29] The "one-third, one-third, one-third" terminology, though convenient, is not entirely accurate—the military departments' shares of the DOD budget, while more or less stable during this period, were not exactly one-third each: the average share for the Department of the Army was about 26%, the average share for the Department of the Navy (which includes both the Navy and Marine Corps) was about 32%, the average share for the Department of the Air Force was about 30%, and the average share for Defense-Wide (the fourth major category of DOD spending) was about 12%. Excluding the Defense-Wide category, which has grown over time, the shares for the three military departments of the remainder of DOD's budget during this period become about 29% for the Department of the Army, about 37% for the Department of the Navy, and about 34% for the Department of the Air Force.

[30] Since the Defense-Wide portion of the budget has grown from just a few percent in the 1950s and 1960s to about 15% in more recent years, including the Defense-Wide category of spending in the calculation can lead to military department shares of the budget in the 1950s and 1960s that are somewhat more elevated compared to those in more recent years, making it more complex to compare the military departments' shares across the entire period of time since the end of the World War II. For this reason, military department shares of the DOD budget cited in this statement are calculated after excluding the Defense-Wide category. The points made in this statement, however, can still made on the basis of a calculation that includes the Defense-Wide category.

Department of the Air Force's share of the non-Defense-Wide DOD budget increased by several percentage points. The Department of the Air Force's share averaged about 45% for the 10-year period FY1956-FY1965, and peaked at more than 47% in FY1957-FY1959.

- For the 11-year period FY2003-FY2013, as a consequence of combat operations in Iraq and Afghanistan, the Department of the Army's share of the non-Defense-Wide DOD budget increased by roughly 10 percentage points. The Department of the Army's share during this period averaged about 39%, and peaked at more than 43% in FY2008. U.S. combat operations in Iraq and Afghanistan during this period reflected the implementation of U.S. national strategy as interpreted by policy makers during those years.

The point of the foregoing is not to argue whether it would be right or wrong to shift more of the DOD budget to the Navy's shipbuilding account or to the Department of the Navy's budget generally. Doing that would require reducing funding for other DOD programs, and policy makers would need to weigh the resulting net impact on overall DOD capabilities. The point, rather, is to note that the allocation of DOD resources is not fixed, that aligning DOD spending with U.S. strategy in coming years could involve changing the allocation by more than a very marginal amount, and that such a changed allocation could provide the funding needed to implement the current 30-year shipbuilding plan. The alternative of assuming at the outset that there is no potential for making anything more than very marginal shifts in the allocation of DOD resources could unnecessarily constrain options available to policy makers and prevent the allocation of DOD resources from being aligned optimally with U.S. strategy.

As an alternative or supplement to the option of altering the allocation of DOD resources among the military departments, the 30-year shipbuilding plan could also become more affordable by taking actions beyond those now being implemented by DOD to control military personnel pay and benefits and reduce what some observers refer to as DOD's overhead or back-office costs. Multiple organizations have made recommendations for such actions in recent years. The Defense Business Board, for example, estimated that at least $200 billion of DOD's enacted budget for FY2010 constituted overhead costs. The board stated, "There has been an explosion of overhead work because the Department has failed to establish adequate controls to keep it in line relative to the size of the warfight," and that "in order to accomplish that work, the Department has applied ever more personnel to those tasks which has added immensely to costs." The board stated further that "whether it's improving the tooth-to-tail ratio; increasing the 'bang for the buck', or converting overhead to combat, Congress and DoD must significantly change their approach," and that DOD "must use the numerous world-class business practices and proven business operations that are applicable to DoD's overhead."[31]

One potential way to interpret the affordability challenge posed by the Navy's 30-year shipbuilding plan is to view it as an invitation by the Navy for policy makers to consider matters such as the alignment between U.S. strategy and the division of DOD resources among the

---

[31] Defense Business Board briefing, "Reducing Overhead and Improving Business Operations, Initial Observations," July 22, 2010, slides 15, 5, and 6, posted online at http://www.govexec.com/pdfs/072210rb1.pdf. See also Defense Business Board, *Modernizing the Military Retirement System*, Report to the Secretary of Defense, Report FY11-05, posted online at http://dbb.defense.gov/Portals/35/Documents/Reports/2011/FY11-5_Modernizing_The_Military_Retirement_System_2011-7.pdf; and Defense Business Board, *Corporate Downsizing Applications for DoD*, Report to the Secretary of Defense, Report FY11-08, posted online at http://dbb.defense.gov/Portals/35/Documents/Reports/2011/FY11-8_Corporate_Downsizing_Applications_for_DoD_2011-7.pdf.

military departments, and the potential for taking actions beyond those now being implemented by DOD to control military personnel pay and benefits and reduce DOD overhead and back-office costs. The Navy's prepared statement for a September 18, 2013, hearing before the House Armed Services Committee on planning for sequestration in FY2014 and the perspectives of the military services on the Strategic Choices and Management Review (SCMR) provides a number of details about reductions in Navy force structure and acquisition programs that could result from constraining DOD's budget to the revised cap levels in the Budget Control Act.[32] These potential reductions do not appear to reflect any substantial shift in the allocation of DOD resources among the military departments, or the taking of actions beyond those already being implemented by DOD to control DOD personnel pay and benefits and reduce DOD overhead and back-office costs. The fact that the Navy in its prepared statement did not choose to discuss the possibility of a changed allocation of DOD resources among the military departments or additional actions to control DOD personnel pay and benefits and reduce DOD overhead and back-office costs does not prevent Congress from considering such possibilities.

Legislative Activity for FY2015

FY2015 Funding Request

The Navy's proposed FY2015 budget requests funding for the procurement of seven new battle force ships (i.e., ships that count against the Navy's goal for achieving and maintaining a fleet of 306 ships). The seven ships include two Virginia-class attack submarines, two DDG-51 class Aegis destroyers, and three Littoral Combat Ships (LCSs). The Navy's proposed FY2015 shipbuilding budget also requests funding for ships that have been procured in prior fiscal years, and ships that are to be procured in future fiscal years.

CRS Reports Tracking Legislation on Specific Navy Shipbuilding Programs

Detailed coverage of legislative activity on certain Navy shipbuilding programs (including funding levels, legislative provisions, and report language) can be found in the following CRS reports:

- CRS Report RS20643, *Navy Ford (CVN-78) Class Aircraft Carrier Program: Background and Issues for Congress*, by Ronald O'Rourke.

  - This report also covers the issue of funding for a refueling complex overhaul (RCOH) for the aircraft carrier *George Washington* (CVN-73).

- CRS Report R41129, *Navy Ohio Replacement (SSBN[X]) Ballistic Missile Submarine Program: Background and Issues for Congress*, by Ronald O'Rourke.

- CRS Report RL32418, *Navy Virginia (SSN-774) Class Attack Submarine Procurement: Background and Issues for Congress*, by Ronald O'Rourke.

---

[32] Statement of Admiral Jonathan Greenert, U.S. Navy, Chief of Naval Operations, Before the House Armed Services Committee on Planning for Sequestration in FY 2014 and Perspectives of the Military Services on the Strategic Choices and Management Review, September 18, 2013, pp. 6-10.

- CRS Report RL32109, *Navy DDG-51 and DDG-1000 Destroyer Programs: Background and Issues for Congress*, by Ronald O'Rourke.

- CRS Report RL33741, *Navy Littoral Combat Ship (LCS) Program: Background and Issues for Congress*, by Ronald O'Rourke.

- CRS Report R43543, *Navy LX(R) Amphibious Ship Program: Background and Issues for Congress*, by Ronald O'Rourke.

  - This report also covers the issue of whether to procure an additional San Antonio (LPD-17) class amphibious ship.

- CRS Report R43546, *Navy TAO(X) Oiler Shipbuilding Program: Background and Issues for Congress*, by Ronald O'Rourke.

  - This report also covers the Navy's proposal, made as part of its FY2015 budget submission, to disestablish the National Defense Sealift Fund (NDSF).

Individual Navy shipbuilding programs that are not covered in detail in the above reports are covered in detail below.

FY2015 National Defense Authorization Act (H.R. 4435/S. 2410)

House (Committee Report)

The House Armed Services Committee, in its report (H.Rept. 113-446 of May 13, 2014) on H.R. 4435, recommends the following changes to the Navy's proposed FY2015 shipbuilding programs:

- an addition of $483.6 million for a refueling complex overhaul (RCOH) of the aircraft carrier *George Washington* (CVN-73);

- a reduction of $54 million to the amount requested for the DDG-1000 destroyer program;

- a reduction of one ship and $450 million to the requested for procurement of LCSs—the recommendation is to procure two LCSs in FY2015, rather than three;

- an addition of $100 million in advance procurement (AP) funding for the procurement of an LCS in a future fiscal year;

- an addition of $800 million for the procurement of an additional LPD-17 class amphibious ship; and

- a reduction of $220 million to the amount requested for the Moored Training Ship (MTS) program, which is a program to convert two older Los Angeles (SSN-688) class attack submarines into moored training platforms for sailors who are learning to use nuclear propulsion plants. (Pages 395-396.)

Section 124 of H.R. 4435 states:

> SEC. 124. LIMITATION ON AVAILABILITY OF FUNDS FOR MOORED TRAINING
> SHIP PROGRAM.

Of the funds authorized to be appropriated by this Act or otherwise made available for fiscal year 2015 for shipbuilding and construction, Navy, for design, conversion, modification, or construction relating to the moored training ship program of the Navy, not more than 80 percent may be obligated or expended until a period of 30 days has elapsed following the date on which the Secretary of Defense certifies to the congressional defense committees that—

(1) the Chairman of the Joint Requirements Oversight Council has reviewed and approved the need for two additional moored training ships;

(2) the Director of Cost Assessment and Program Evaluation has reviewed and certified the cost estimates of the moored training ship program; and

(3) the Under Secretary of Defense for Acquisition, Technology, and Logistics has reviewed and approved the budget, schedule, and construction plans for such two additional moored training ships.

Regarding the Moored Training Ship Program addressed in the above provision, H.Rept. 113-446 states:

Moored Training Ship

The budget request contained $801.7 million in Shipbuilding and Conversion, Navy, for the Moored Training Ship program.

The committee notes that the Moored Training Ship program is intended to convert two decommissioned nuclear attack submarines into training platforms for nuclear propulsion crew members. The committee also notes that this program has experienced a $556.8 million cost overrun for the two conversions compared to fiscal year 2014 budget projections, and that this represents an 34 percent cost increase. The committee further notes that $229.7 million of this cost increase is included in the fiscal year 2015 budget request. While the committee understands that the Moored Training Ship program is not a formal acquisition program, the committee remains concerned that the 34 percent cost increase would be significantly over the critical cost growth threshold for major defense acquisition programs, established pursuant to section 2433, title 10, United States Code, also known as a "Nunn-McCurdy breach". As a result, elsewhere in this Act, the committee includes a provision that would require a review to be provided to Congress similar to that required for a "Nunn-McCurdy breach".

The committee recommends $572.0 million, a decrease of $229.7 million, in shipbuilding and conversion, Navy, for the Moored Training Ship program. (Page 30)

Section 1021 of H.R. 4435 as reported states:

SEC. 1021. DEFINITION OF COMBATANT AND SUPPORT VESSEL FOR PURPOSES OF THE ANNUAL PLAN AND CERTIFICATION RELATING TO BUDGETING FOR CONSTRUCTION OF NAVAL VESSELS.

Section 231(f) of title 10, United States Code, is amended by adding at the end the following new paragraph:

`(4) The term `combatant and support vessel' means any commissioned ship built or armed for naval combat or any naval ship designed to provide support to combatant ships and other naval operations. Such term does not include patrol coastal ships, non-commissioned combatant craft specifically designed for combat roles, or ships that are designated for potential mobilization.'.

Section 1026 of H.R. 4435 as reported states:

SEC. 1026. AVAILABILITY OF FUNDS FOR RETIREMENT OR INACTIVATION OF TICONDEROGA CLASS CRUISERS OR DOCK LANDING SHIPS.

(a) Limitation on the Availability of Funds- Except as otherwise provided in this section, none of the funds authorized to be appropriated by this Act or otherwise made available for the Department of Defense for fiscal year 2015 may be obligated or expended to retire, prepare to retire, inactivate, or place in storage a cruiser or dock landing ship.

(b) Cruiser Upgrades- As provided by section 8107 of the Consolidated Appropriations Act, 2014 (P.L. 113-76), the Secretary of the Navy shall begin the upgrade of two cruisers during fiscal year 2015, including—

(1) hull, mechanical, and electrical upgrades; and

(2) combat systems modernizations.

Regarding the cruisers and amphibious ships addressed in the above provision, H.Rept. 113-446 states:

Phased Modernization of Certain Navy Ships

In March 2014, the Navy proposed to reduce its operational force structure of Ticonderoga-class cruisers and amphibious dock landing ships (LSD). The Navy plans to take 14 ships out of their normal deployment rotations and place them in long-term phased modernization and maintenance to extend the expected service life of the ships. According to the Navy, this plan will allow it to retain the 11 cruisers and 3 amphibious ships through the 2030s and into the 2040s.

The committee is concerned about the Navy's plan to reduce its battle force structure by 14 ships, especially in light of shortfalls in the force structure necessary to meet the requirements of the National Military Strategy. Additionally, the committee notes that while the Navy places Military Sealift Command ships in reduced operating status, or ROS, on a regular basis, surface combatant and amphibious ships are more complex and their crews need more training before they can be certified as being ready for deployment and major combat operations. Further, the Navy states it has not reactivated any surface combatant ships from long-term protective storage since the 1980s.

Therefore, the committee directs the Comptroller General of the United States to report to the congressional defense committees by March 1, 2015, on the extent to which the Navy has identified:

(1) The potential costs and cost savings associated with the Navy's phased modernization plan for the 11 cruisers and 3 LSDs;

(2) The operational benefits and risks associated with this long-term plan; and

(3) The costs, savings, benefits, and risks of any alternate plans that were considered before putting forth the Navy's current plan. (Pages 210-211)

H.Rept. 113-446 also states:

Joint High Speed Vessel

The committee is aware of the premium that the Department of Defense places on the ability of U.S. military forces to deploy quickly to a full spectrum of engagements. In addition, the Department values the ability of U.S. forces to debark and embark in a wide range of port environments, from modern to austere.

The committee notes that the Joint High Speed Vessel (JHSV), crewed by Military Sealift Command mariners, has demonstrated the ability to transport military forces, as well as humanitarian relief personnel and materiel, in a manner that is responsive, deployable, agile, versatile, and sustainable. The USNS Spearhead (JHSV–1) is currently deployed to the U.S. 6th Fleet area of responsibility.

The JHSV is designed to transport 600 short tons of military cargo 1,200 nautical miles at an average speed of 35 knots in sea state 3. JHSVs support Navy Expeditionary Combat Command and riverine forces, theater cooperating missions, Seabees, and Marine Corps and Army transportation. The original procurement objective for the JHSV was 18 ships. This procurement number was lowered to 10 JHSVs as part of the budget request for fiscal year 2013.

The committee notes that the JHSV has the ability to support multiple branches of the military services, provide high-speed intra-theater sealift, operate in littoral environments and austere port environments, and support humanitarian and disaster relief activities. The committee also notes that the ship's construction line is still operational. For these reasons, the committee directs the Secretary of the Navy to submit a report to the congressional defense committees by April 1, 2015, on the operational benefits and cost savings associated with continuing to procure JHSVs. The report should specifically address the costs and benefits of buying the eight additional JHSVs that were originally part of the program. (Page 29)

H.Rept. 113-446 also states:

Mobile Landing Platform Afloat Forward Staging Base

The committee notes that the most recent 30-year shipbuilding plan projects a requirement for a third Mobile Landing Platform (MLP) Afloat Forward Staging Base (AFSB) variant ship in fiscal year 2017. Full funding for the second MLP AFSB ship was provided in fiscal year 2014. No advance procurement funds for the third MLP AFSB ship are currently programmed in either fiscal year 2015 or fiscal year 2016. Considering the expanded requirement for the MLP AFSB variant ships and the success of the ongoing shipbuilding program, the committee is concerned that a 3-year procurement gap between ships will increase costs, impact the industrial base, and delay delivery of important capabilities. Therefore, the committee encourages the Secretary of the Navy to explore possible approaches to minimize a production break between ships, including advance procurement funding, for the third AFSB ship. (Page 30)

H.Rept. 113-446 also states:

Comptroller General Review of Forward Deployed Naval Forces and Associated
Sustainment Issues

Forward presence is critical to the Navy's goals of building partnerships, deterring aggression without escalation, defusing threats, and containing conflict without regional disruption. Naval forces provide forward presence through a combination of rotational deployments from the United States, Forward Deployed Naval Forces (FDNF) in Japan, Guam, the Kingdom of Spain, and the Italian Republic, and forward stationing ships in places such as the Kingdom of Bahrain, the Republic of Singapore, and Diego Garcia. The Navy's ability to implement these concepts depends on U.S. bases and strategic partnerships overseas that provide places where forces can rest, repair, refuel, and resupply. In the FDNF construct, the ships, crews and families all reside in the host nation. This construct is in contrast to forward stationing, where the ship's families reside in the United States and the crew rotates to the ship's overseas location for deployment.

The committee seeks a more detailed understanding of the Navy's decision-making process to designate ships to be either FDNF or forward stationed and the relative costs and benefits of each approach. The committee directs the Comptroller General of the United States to provide a report to the congressional defense committees by February 27, 2015. The report should include a review and analysis of:

(1) The Navy's process for determining the homeport locations of naval vessels, including FDNF;

(2) The Navy's process for stationing naval vessels outside the United States;

(3) How the Navy calculates deployment costs of vessels homeported inside and outside the United States;

(4) The extent to which the Navy has utilized rotational crewing to meet forward presence requirements;

(5) The operational availability achieved by rotational crewing, the savings achieved, and the limitations associated with directed rotational crewing;

(6) The operational support and sustainment effects of deploying U.S.-based vessels to a forward operating station as opposed to homeporting vessels outside the United States, including costs of complying with section 7310 of title 10, United States Code, maintenance requirements;

(7) The infrastructure requirements, as well as host-nation acceptance requirements to ensure the assets are received overseas; and

(8) Any other issue that the Comptroller General determines appropriate. (Pages 111-112)

H.Rept. 113-446 also states:

Force Structure Assessment

The committee notes that the Secretary of the Navy conducted a Force Structure Assessment in 2012 that determined the proposed composition of Navy surface and subsurface vessels. This latest Force Structure Assessment determined that an overall Navy fleet of 306 ships would be necessary to support the overall defense strategy. Since the release of the 2012 Force Structure Assessment, the Secretary of Defense released the 2014 Quadrennial Defense Review which determined, in part, the requirement for 11 aircraft carriers and 92 large surface combatants. Therefore, the committee directs the Secretary of the Navy to update the most recent Force Structure Assessment and to submit it to the congressional defense committees by March 1, 2015. (Pages 205-206)

House (Floor Action)

On May 21, 2014, as part of its consideration of H.R. 4435, the House agreed to by voice vote H.Amdt. 682, an en bloc amendment consisting of several amendments printed in H.Rept. 113-460 of May 21 (legislative day, May 20), 2014, a report providing for further consideration of H.R. 4435. One of these was amendment number 161 from H.Rept. 113-60, which increased by $20 million the amount authorized for the Defense Health Program and identified $20 million in offsets, including a $10 million reduction from the amounted authorized for the Shipbuilding and Conversion, Navy (SCN) account.

Senate

The Senate Armed Services Committee, in its report (S.Rept. 113-176 of June 2, 2014) on S. 2410, recommends the following changes to the Navy's proposed FY2015 shipbuilding programs:

- a transfer from the Operation and Maintenance, Navy (OMN) account to the Shipbuilding and Conversion, Navy (SCN) account of the Navy's request for $46 million in FY2015 funding for defueling the aircraft carrier *George Washington* (CVN-73), so as to support a refueling complex overhaul (RCOH) for that ship; and

- a transfer from the Research, Development, Test and Evaluation, Navy (RDTEN) account to the SCN account of the Navy's request for $45 million in FY2015 funding for a service life extension program (SLEP) for the Navy's air-cushioned landing craft (LCAC). (Pages 323-324.)

Section 1022 of S. 2410 as reported states:

SEC. 1022. AVAILABILITY OF FUNDS FOR RETIREMENT OR INACTIVATION OF TICONDEROGA CLASS CRUISERS OR DOCK LANDING SHIPS.

(a) Limitation on Availability of Funds-

(1) IN GENERAL- Except as otherwise provided in this section, none of the funds authorized to be appropriated or otherwise made available for the Department of Defense by this Act or the National Defense Authorization Act for Fiscal Year 2014 (P.L. 113-66) may be obligated or expended to retire, prepare to retire, inactivate, or place in storage a cruiser or dock landing ship.

(2) USE OF SMOSF FUNDS- Funds in the Ship, Modernization, Operations, and Sustainment Fund (SMOSF) may be used only for 11 Ticonderoga-class cruisers (CG 63 through CG 73) and 3 dock landing ships (LSD 41, LSD 42, and LSD 46). The Secretary of the Navy may use such funds only to man, operate, equip, sustain, and modernize such vessels.

(b) Phased Modernization of Ticonderoga Class Cruisers and Dock Landing Ships- The Secretary of the Navy shall retain 22 Ticonderoga-class cruisers (CGs) and 12 Whidbey Island/Harpers Ferry-class dock landing ships (LSDs) until the end of their expected service lives, as follows:

(1) OPERATIONAL FORCES- The naval combat forces of the Navy shall include not less than 11 operational cruisers (CG 52 through CG 62) and 11 operational dock landing ships (all members of the LSD 41 class, except LSD 41, LSD, 42 and LSD 46). For purposes of this paragraph, a cruiser or dock landing ship is operational if such vessel is available for worldwide deployment other than during routine or scheduled maintenance or repair.

(2) PHASED MODERNIZATION- The Secretary may conduct phased modernization of the cruisers and dock landing ships for which funds in the Ship, Modernization, Operations, and Sustainment Fund are authorized to be available pursuant to subsection (a)(2). During a phased modernization period, the Secretary may reduce manning on such vessels to the minimal level necessary to ensure the safety and security of such vessels and to retain critical skills.

(3) END OF SERVICE AND TRANSITION FROM PHASED MODERNIZATION TO OPERATIONAL FORCES- Cruisers covered by paragraph (1) may only be decommissioned when replaced by one of the cruisers for which the Navy has conducted a phased modernization using funds in the Ship, Modernization, Operations, and Sustainment Fund as described in paragraph (2). After being reintroduced into the operational fleet, the cruisers modernized as described in paragraph (2) may be decommissioned individually upon reaching the end of their expected service life, excluding time spent in a phased modernization status under paragraph (2). After being reintroduced into the operational fleet, the dock landing ships modernized as described in paragraph (2) may be decommissioned upon reaching the end of their expected service life, excluded time spent in a phased modernization status under paragraph (2).

(c) Requirements and Limitations on Phased Modernization-

(1) REQUIREMENTS- During the period of phased modernization under subsection (b)(2) of the vessels specified in subsection (a)(2), the Secretary of the Navy shall--

(A) continue to maintain the vessels in a manner that will ensure the ability of the vessels to reenter the operational fleet;

(B) conduct planning activities to ensure scheduled and deferred maintenance and modernization work items are identified and included in maintenance availability work packages;

(C) conduct hull, mechanical, and electrical (HM&E) and combat system modernization necessary to achieve a service life of 40 years;

(D) in the case of the cruisers, schedule completion of maintenance and modernization, including required testing and crew training, to replace on a one-for-one basis, active cruisers that will be decommissioned upon reaching the end of their expected service life;

(E) ensure adequate funds are available to execute phased modernization activities for all the vessels.

(2) LIMITATIONS- During the period of phased modernization under subsection (b)(2) of the vessels specified in subsection (a)(2), the Secretary may not--

(A) permit removal or cannibalization of equipment or systems to support operational vessels, other than--

(i) rotatable pool equipment; and

(ii) equipment or systems necessary to support urgent operational requirements (but only with the approval of the Secretary of Defense); or

(B) make any irreversible modifications that will prohibit the vessel from reentering the operational fleet.

(d) Authority To Enter Into Economic Order Quantity Contracts- The Secretary of the Navy may enter into a so-called `economic order quantity' contracts with private shipyards for ship maintenance and modernization, and with private industry for equipment procurement for the phased modernization under subsection (b)(2) of the vessels specified in subsection (a)(2).

(e) Reports-

(1) IN GENERAL- At the same time as the submittal to Congress of the budget of the President under section 1105 of title 31, United States, for each fiscal year in which activities under the phased modernization of vessels will be carried out under this section, the Secretary of the Navy shall submit to the congressional defense committees a written report on the status of the phased modernization of vessels under this section.

(2) ELEMENTS- Each report under this subsection shall include the following:

(A) The status of phased modernization efforts, including availability schedules, equipment procurement schedules, and by-fiscal year funding requirements.

(B) The readiness, and operational and manning status of each vessel to be undergoing phased modernization under this section during the fiscal year covered by such report.

(C) The current material condition assessment for each such vessel.

(D) A list of rotatable pool equipment that is identified across the whole class of cruisers to support operations on a continuing basis.

(E) A list of equipment, other than rotatable pool equipment and components incidental to performing maintenance, removed from each such vessel, including a justification for the removal, the disposition of the equipment, and plan for restoration of the equipment.

(F) A detailed plan for obligations and expenditures by vessel for the fiscal year beginning in the year of such report, and projections of obligations by vessel by fiscal year for the remaining time a vessel is in the phased modernization program.

(G) A statement of the funding required during the fiscal year beginning in the year of such report to ensure the Ship, Modernization, Operations, and Sustainment Fund account has adequate resources to execute the plan under subparagraph (F) in the execution fiscal year and the following fiscal year.

(3) NOTICE ON VARIANCE FROM PLAN- Not later than 30 days before executing any material deviation from a plan under paragraph (2)(F) for a fiscal year, the Secretary shall notify the congressional defense committees in writing of such deviation from the plan.

(f) Repeal of Superseded Limitation- Section 1023 of the National Defense Authorization Act for Fiscal Year 2014 (127 Stat. 846) is repealed.

Regarding Section 1022, S.Rept. 113-176 states:

Availability of funds for retirement or inactivation of Ticonderoga class cruisers or dock landing ships (sec. 1022)

The committee recommends a provision that would establish rules under which the Navy could use resources in the Ship, Modernization, Operations, and Sustainment Fund (SMOSF) to implement a plan to: (1) Retain 11 Ticonderoga-class cruisers and 9 Whidbey Island-class and Harpers Ferry-class dock landing ships in active service; (2) Temporarily inactivate 11 Ticonderoga-class cruisers and 3 Whidbey Island-class dock landing ships; (3) Modernize the inactivated ships during the period of their inactivation; and (4) Reactivate those ships to replace cruisers and dock landing ships retiring at the end of their expected service lives.

The provision would require that the Secretary of the Navy retain the cruisers and dock landing ships until the end of their ex pected service lives, and use SMOSF only to sustain and modernize the vessels.

The provision would also require the Secretary of the Navy to submit an annual report with the budget request. The report would describe the status of the SMOSF, including specific financial information, such as starting and ending fiscal year corpus balances, providing a detailed obligation and expenditure plan by vessel, and including information detailing all transfers into and out of the SMOSF by appropriation account.

The committee further directs the Secretary to ensure that the annual budget justification material for the SMOSF include detailed information at the vessel level. In addition, the committee directs the Defense Finance and Accounting Service to provide execution reports for the SMOSF that treats each vessel like a line item within the SMOSF. (Pages 165-166)

S.Rept. 113-176 also states:

Report on the Navy's shipbuilding industrial base

In testimony before the Seapower Subcommittee of this committee, the Assistant Secretary of the Navy for Research, Development and Acquisition expressed concern about the fragility of the Navy's shipbuilding industrial base. Other Navy officials, including the Secretary of the Navy and the Chief of Naval Operations have expressed similar concerns. The committee shares these concerns and requests the Secretary of the Navy, in conjunction with the Under Secretary of Defense for Acquisitions, Technology, and Logistics, provide a report on the state of the Navy's shipbuilding industrial base not later than February 1, 2015. The report should contain the following:

(1) A comparison of shipyard capacities and capabilities with projected shipbuilding workloads, and challenges this may produce in coming years in terms of capacity utilization and preservation of key design and construction skills.

(2) Investments the shipyards have made in recent years to modernize their production facilities and to recruit, train, and retain their workers, and any challenges the shipyards may face in doing this in coming years.

(3) Investments the shipyards could make to achieve cost reductions on Navy programs or to position the yards to survive a number of years on reduced Navy orders.

(4) The shipyards' construction processes and methods, and how these compare to best practices in shipyards around the world.

(5) The prospects, by ship type, for using competition in the design and construction of Navy ships in coming years.

(6) A comparison of supplier capacities and capabilities with projected shipbuilding workloads, and challenges this may produce in coming years in terms of capacity utilization and preservation of key suppliers.

(7) A comparison of shipbuilding research and development investments with projected shipbuilding workloads, and any challenges that deficiencies in investment may produce in future years in utilizing capacity, preserving of key skills, and continuing innovation.

(8) An analysis of the risks to the shipbuilding industrial base in the Navy's shipbuilding plan in the 2015 future years defense program, and the risks to the industrial base if Congress does not amend the Budget Control Act to increase budget levels for the Department of Defense before fiscal year 2016.

(9) A comprehensive funding section that includes:

(a) An itemized listing of funds budgeted for support of the shipbuilding industrial base. This is to include all applicable Navy and Defense-wide appropriations. Detail must be by fiscal year at the Appropriation, line item/program element-project level with a description of the effort. Detail should be provided over the future years defense program and include up to 10 years of prior fiscal year actuals. This detailed listing is to specifically include funding contained in current shipbuilding programs (detail design/plans), as well as the research and development funding for preliminary and contract design program elements, and any applicable science and technology funding, as well as applicable funding from the Industrial Preparedness and Manufacturing Technology programs.

(b) Any recommendations in the report for additional funding should be identified at the same level of detail as described in the subsection above.

(c) The report funding summary should also provide information on applicable efforts from other related agencies, such as the Department of Transportation, the Maritime Administration, and the Coast Guard. (Pages 31-32)

Appendix A. Comparing Past Ship Force Levels to Current or Potential Future Ship Force Levels

In assessing the appropriateness of the current or potential future number of ships in the Navy, observers sometimes compare that number to historical figures for total Navy fleet size. Historical figures for total fleet size, however, can be a problematic yardstick for assessing the appropriateness of the current or potential future number of ships in the Navy, particularly if the historical figures are more than a few years old, because

- the missions to be performed by the Navy, the mix of ships that make up the Navy, and the technologies that are available to Navy ships for performing missions all change over time; and

- the number of ships in the fleet in an earlier year might itself have been inappropriate (i.e., not enough or more than enough) for the meeting the Navy's mission requirements in that year.

Regarding the first bullet point above, the Navy, for example, reached a late-Cold War peak of 568 battle force ships at the end of FY1987,[33] and as of April 7, 2014, included a total of 289 battle force ships. The FY1987 fleet, however, was intended to meet a set of mission requirements that focused on countering Soviet naval forces at sea during a potential multi-theater NATO-Warsaw Pact conflict, while the April 2014 fleet is intended to meet a considerably different set of mission requirements centered on influencing events ashore by countering both land- and sea-based military forces of potential regional threats other than Russia, including improved Chinese military forces and non-state terrorist organizations. In addition, the Navy of FY1987 differed substantially from the April 2014 fleet in areas such as profusion of precision-guided air-delivered weapons, numbers of Tomahawk-capable ships, and the sophistication of C4ISR systems and networking capabilities.[34]

In coming years, Navy missions may shift again, and the capabilities of Navy ships will likely have changed further by that time due to developments such as more comprehensive implementation of networking technology, increased use of ship-based unmanned vehicles, and the potential fielding of new types of weapons such as lasers or electromagnetic rail guns.

The 568-ship fleet of FY1987 may or may not have been capable of performing its stated missions; the 289-ship fleet of April 2014 may or may not be capable of performing its stated missions; and a fleet years from now with a certain number of ships may or may not be capable of

---

[33] Some publications have stated that the Navy reached a peak of 594 ships at the end of FY1987. This figure, however, is the total number of active ships in the fleet, which is not the same as the total number of battle force ships. The battle force ships figure is the number used in government discussions of the size of the Navy. In recent years, the total number of active ships has been larger than the total number of battle force ships. For example, the Naval History and Heritage Command (formerly the Naval Historical Center) states that as of November 16, 2001, the Navy included a total of 337 active ships, while the Navy states that as of November 19, 2001, the Navy included a total of 317 battle force ships. Comparing the total number of active ships in one year to the total number of battle force ships in another year is thus an apples-to-oranges comparison that in this case overstates the decline since FY1987 in the number of ships in the Navy. As a general rule to avoid potential statistical distortions, comparisons of the number of ships in the Navy over time should use, whenever possible, a single counting method.

[34] C4ISR stands for command and control, communications, computers, intelligence, surveillance, and reconnaissance.

performing its stated missions. Given changes over time in mission requirements, ship mixes, and technologies, however, these three issues are to a substantial degree independent of one another.

For similar reasons, trends over time in the total number of ships in the Navy are not necessarily a reliable indicator of the direction of change in the fleet's ability to perform its stated missions. An increasing number of ships in the fleet might not necessarily mean that the fleet's ability to perform its stated missions is increasing, because the fleet's mission requirements might be increasing more rapidly than ship numbers and average ship capability. Similarly, a decreasing number of ships in the fleet might not necessarily mean that the fleet's ability to perform stated missions is decreasing, because the fleet's mission requirements might be declining more rapidly than numbers of ships, or because average ship capability and the percentage of time that ships are in deployed locations might be increasing quickly enough to more than offset reductions in total ship numbers.

Regarding the second of the two bullet points above, it can be noted that comparisons of the size of the fleet today with the size of the fleet in earlier years rarely appear to consider whether the fleet was appropriately sized in those earlier years (and therefore potentially suitable as a yardstick of comparison), even though it is quite possible that the fleet in those earlier years might not have been appropriately sized, and even though there might have been differences of opinion among observers at that time regarding that question. Just as it might not be prudent for observers years from now to tacitly assume that the 289-ship of April 2014 was appropriately sized for meeting the mission requirements of 2013, even though there currently are differences of opinion among observers on that question (as reflected, for example, in **Table 7**) simply because a figure of 289 ships appears in the historical records for 2014, so, too, might it not be prudent for observers today to tacitly assume that the number of ships of the Navy in an earlier year was appropriate for meeting the Navy's mission requirements that year, even though there might have been differences of opinion among observers at that time regarding that question, simply because the size of the Navy in that year appears in a table like **Table C-1**.

Previous Navy force structure plans, such as those shown in **Table 1**, might provide some insight into the potential adequacy of a proposed new force-structure plan, but changes over time in mission requirements, technologies available to ships for performing missions, and other force-planning factors, as well as the possibility that earlier force-structure plans might not have been appropriate for meeting the mission demands of their times, suggest that some caution should be applied in using past force structure plans for this purpose, particularly if those past force structure plans are more than a few years old. The Reagan-era plan for a 600-ship Navy, for example, was designed for a Cold War set of missions focusing on countering Soviet naval forces at sea, which is not an appropriate basis for planning the Navy today, and there was considerable debate during those years as to the appropriateness of the 600-ship goal.[35]

---

[35] Navy force structure plans that predate those shown in **Table 1** include the Reagan-era 600-ship plan of the 1980s, the Base Force fleet of more than 400 ships planned during the final two years of the George H. W. Bush Administration, the 346-ship fleet from the Clinton Administration's 1993 Bottom-Up Review (or BUR, sometimes also called Base Force II), and the 310-ship fleet of the Clinton Administration's 1997 QDR. The table below summarizes some key features of these plans.

Features of Recent Navy Force Structure Plans

Plan	600-ship	Base Force	1993 BUR	1997 QDR
Total ships	~600	~450/416[a]	346	~305/310[b]
Attack submarines	100	80/~55[c]	45-55	50/55[d]

(continued...)

Appendix B. Independent Panel Assessment of 2010 QDR

The law that requires DOD to perform QDRs once every four years (10 U.S.C. 118) states that the results of each QDR shall be assessed by an independent panel. The report of the independent panel that assessed the 2010 QDR was released on July 29, 2010. The independent panel's report recommended a Navy of 346 ships, including 11 aircraft carriers and 55 attack submarines.[36] The report stated the following, among other things:

- "The QDR should reflect current commitments, but it must also plan effectively for potential threats that could arise over the next 20 years.... we believe the 2010 QDR did not accord sufficient priority to the need to counter anti-access challenges, strengthen homeland defense (including our defense against cyber threats), and conduct post-conflict stabilization missions." (Page 54)

- "In this remarkable period of change, global security will still depend upon an American presence capable of unimpeded access to all international areas of the Pacific region. In an environment of 'anti-access strategies,' and assertions to create unique 'economic and security zones of influence,' America's rightful and historic presence will be critical. To preserve our interests, the United States will need to retain the ability to transit freely the areas of the Western Pacific for security and economic reasons. Our allies also depend on us to be fully present in the Asia-Pacific as a promoter of stability and to ensure the free flow of commerce. A robust U.S. force structure, largely rooted in maritime strategy but including other necessary capabilities, will be essential." (Page 51)

- "The United States will need agile forces capable of operating against the full range of potential contingencies. However, the need to deal with irregular and hybrid threats will tend to drive the size and shape of ground forces for years to

(...continued)				
Aircraft carriers	15[e]	12	11+1[f]	11+1[f]
Surface combatants	242/228[g]	~150	~124	116
Amphibious ships	~75[h]	51[i]	41[i]	36[i]

Source: Prepared by CRS based on DOD and U.S. Navy data.
a. Commonly referred to as 450-ship plan, but called for decreasing to 416 ships by end of FY1999.
b. Original total of about 305 ships was increased to about 310 due to increase in number of attack submarines to 55 from 50.
c. Plan originally included 80 attack submarines, but this was later reduced to about 55.
d. Plan originally included 50 attack submarines but this was later increased to 55.
e. Plus one additional aircraft carrier in the service life extension program (SLEP).
f. Eleven active carriers plus one operational reserve carrier.
g. Plan originally included 242 surface combatants but this was later reduced to 228.
h. Number needed to lift assault echelons of one Marine Expeditionary Force (MEF) plus one Marine Expeditionary Brigade (MEB).
i. Number needed to lift assault echelons of 2.5 MEBs. Changing numbers needed to meet this goal reflect in part changes in the design and capabilities of amphibious ships.

[36] Stephen J. Hadley and William J. Perry, co-chairmen, et al, *The QDR in Perspective: Meeting America's National Security Needs In the 21st Century, The Final Report of the Quadrennial Defense Review Independent Panel*, Washington, 2010, Figure 3-2 on page 58.

come, whereas the need to continue to be fully present in Asia and the Pacific and other areas of interest will do the same for naval and air forces." (Page 55)

- "The force structure in the Asia-Pacific needs to be increased. In order to preserve U.S. interests, the United States will need to retain the ability to transit freely the areas of the Western Pacific for security and economic reasons. The United States must be fully present in the Asia-Pacific region to protect American lives and territory, ensure the free flow of commerce, maintain stability, and defend our allies in the region. A robust U.S. force structure, one that is largely rooted in maritime strategy and includes other necessary capabilities, will be essential." (Page 66)

- "Force structure must be strengthened in a number of areas to address the need to counter anti-access challenges, strengthen homeland defense (including defense against cyber threats), and conduct post-conflict stabilization missions: First, as a Pacific power, the U.S. presence in Asia has underwritten the regional stability that has enabled India and China to emerge as rising economic powers. The United States should plan on continuing that role for the indefinite future. The Panel remains concerned that the QDR force structure may not be sufficient to assure others that the United States can meet its treaty commitments in the face of China's increased military capabilities. Therefore, we recommend an increased priority on defeating anti-access and area-denial threats. This will involve acquiring new capabilities, and, as Secretary Gates has urged, developing innovative concepts for their use. Specifically, we believe the United States must fully fund the modernization of its surface fleet. We also believe the United States must be able to deny an adversary sanctuary by providing persistent surveillance, tracking, and rapid engagement with high-volume precision strike. That is why the Panel supports an increase in investment in long-range strike systems and their associated sensors. In addition, U.S. forces must develop and demonstrate the ability to operate in an information-denied environment." (Pages 59-60)

- "To compete effectively, the U.S. military must continue to develop new conceptual approaches to dealing with operational challenges, like the Capstone Concept for Joint Operations (CCJO). The Navy and Air Force's effort to develop an Air-Sea Battle concept is one example of an approach to deal with the growing anti-access challenge. It will be necessary to invest in modernized capabilities to make this happen. The Chief of Naval Operations and Chief of Staff of the Air Force deserve support in this effort, and the Panel recommends the other military services be brought into the concept when appropriate." (Page 51; a similar passage appears on page 67)

In recommending a Navy of 346 ships, the independent panel's report cited the 1993 Bottom-Up Review (BUR) of U.S. defense plans and policies. **Table B-1** compares the Navy's 306-ship goal of March 2012 to the 346-ship Navy recommended in the 1993 BUR (as detailed partly in subsequent Navy testimony and publications) and the ship force levels recommended in the independent panel report.

Table B-1. Comparison of Navy's 306-ship goal, Navy Plan from 1993 BUR, and Navy Plan from 2010 QDR Review Panel

Ship Type	Navy's 306-ship goal of March 2012	Bottom-Up Review (BUR) (1993)	2010 QDR Independent Review Panel (July 2010)
SSBNs	12-14	18	14
		(SSBN force was later reduced to 14 as a result of the 1994 Nuclear Posture Review)	
SSGNs	0-4	0	4
		(SSGN program did not yet exist)	
SSNs	~48	45 to 55	55
		(55 in FY99, with a long-term goal of about 45)	
Aircraft carriers	11 active	11 active + 1 operational/reserve	11 active
Surface combatants	~145	124	n/a
		(114 active + 10 frigates in Naval Reserve Force; a total of 110-116 active ships was also cited)	
Cruisers and destroyers	*~90*	*n/a*	*n/a*
Frigates	*0*	*n/a*	*n/a*
	(to be replaced by LCSs)		
LCSs	*~55*	*0*	*n/a*
		(LCS program did not exist)	
Amphibious ships	~32	41	n/a
	(30 operational ships needed to lift 2.0 MEBs)	(Enough to lift 2.5 MEBs)	
Dedicated mine warfare ships	0	26	n/a
	(to be replaced by LCSs)	(LCS program did not exist)	
CLF ships	~29	43	n/a
Support ships	~33	22	n/a
TOTAL ships	**~306**	**346**	**346**
		(numbers above add to 331-341)[a]	

Source: Table prepared by CRS. ***Sources for 1993 Bottom-Up Review:*** Department of Defense, *Report on the Bottom-Up Review*, October 1993, Figure 7 on page 28; Department of the Navy, *Highlights of the FY 1995 Department of the Navy Budget*, February 1994, p. 1; Department of the Navy, *Force 2001, A Program Guide to the U.S. Navy*, 1994 edition, p. 15; Statement of VADM T. Joseph Lopez, U.S. Navy, Deputy Chief of Naval Operations (Resources, Warfare Requirements & Assessments), Testimony to the Military Forces and Personnel Subcommittee of the House Armed Services Committee, March 22, 1994, pp. 2-5. ***Source for independent panel report:*** Stephen J. Hadley and William J. Perry, co-chairmen, et al., *The QDR in Perspective: Meeting*

America's National Security Needs In the 21st Century, The Final Report of the Quadrennial Defense Review Independent Panel, Washington, 2010, Figure 3-2 on pages 58-59.

Notes: n/a is not addressed in the report. **SSBN** is nuclear-powered ballistic missile submarine; **SSGN** is nuclear-powered cruise missile and special operations forces submarine; **SSN** is nuclear-powered attack submarine; **LCS** is Littoral Combat Ship; **MPF(F)** is Maritime Prepositioning Force (Future) ship; **CLF** is combat logistics force (i.e., resupply) ship; **MEB** is Marine Expeditionary Brigade.

a.   The Navy testified in 1994 that the planned number was adjusted from 346 to 330 to reflect reductions in numbers of tenders and early retirements of some older amphibious ships.

In a letter dated August 11, 2010, Secretary of Defense Robert Gates provided his comments on the independent panel's report. The letter stated in part:

> I completely agree with the Panel that a strong navy is essential; however, I disagree with the Panel's recommendation that DoD should establish the 1993 Bottom Up Review's (BUR's) fleet of 346 ships as the objective target. That number was a simple projection of the then-planned size of [the] Navy in FY 1999, not a reflection of 21st century, steady-state requirements. The fleet described in the 2010 QDR report, with its overall target of 313 to 321 ships, has roughly the same number of aircraft carriers, nuclear-powered attack submarines, surface combatants, mine warfare vessels, and amphibious ships as the larger BUR fleet. The main difference between the two fleets is in the numbers of combat logistics, mobile logistics, and support ships. Although it is true that the 2010 fleet includes fewer of these ships, they are all now more efficiently manned and operated by the Military Sealift Command and meet all of DoD's requirements....
>
> I agree with the Panel's general conclusion that DoD ought to enhance its overall posture and capabilities in the Asia-Pacific region. As I outlined in my speech at the Naval War College in April 2009, "to carry out the missions we may face in the future... we will need numbers, speed, and the ability to operate in shallow waters." So as the Air-Sea battle concept development reaches maturation, and as DoD's review of global defense posture continues, I will be looking for ways to meet plausible security threats while emphasizing sustained forward presence – particularly in the Pacific.[37]

[37] Letter dated August 11, 2010, from Secretary of Defense Robert Gates to the chairmen of the House and Senate Armed Services and Appropriations Committees, pp. 3 and 4. The ellipsis in the second paragraph appears in the letter.

Appendix C. Size of the Navy and Navy Shipbuilding Rate

Size of the Navy

Table C-1 shows the size of the Navy in terms of total number of ships since FY1948; the numbers shown in the table reflect changes over time in the rules specifying which ships count toward the total. Differing counting rules result in differing totals, and for certain years, figures reflecting more than one set of counting rules are available. Figures in the table for FY1978 and subsequent years reflect the battle force ships counting method, which is the set of counting rules established in the early 1980s for public policy discussions of the size of the Navy.

As shown in the table, the total number of battle force ships in the Navy reached a late-Cold War peak of 568 at the end of FY1987 and began declining thereafter.[38] The Navy fell below 300 battle force ships in August 2003 and included 289 battle force ships as of April 7, 2014.

As discussed in **Appendix A**, historical figures for total fleet size might not be a reliable yardstick for assessing the appropriateness of proposals for the future size and structure of the Navy, particularly if the historical figures are more than a few years old, because the missions to be performed by the Navy, the mix of ships that make up the Navy, and the technologies that are available to Navy ships for performing missions all change over time, and because the number of ships in the fleet in an earlier year might itself have been inappropriate (i.e., not enough or more than enough) for the meeting the Navy's mission requirements in that year.

For similar reasons, trends over time in the total number of ships in the Navy are not necessarily a reliable indicator of the direction of change in the fleet's ability to perform its stated missions. An increasing number of ships in the fleet might not necessarily mean that the fleet's ability to perform its stated missions is increasing, because the fleet's mission requirements might be increasing more rapidly than ship numbers and average ship capability. Similarly, a decreasing number of ships in the fleet might not necessarily mean that the fleet's ability to perform stated missions is decreasing, because the fleet's mission requirements might be declining more rapidly than numbers of ships, or because average ship capability and the percentage of time that ships are in deployed locations might be increasing quickly enough to more than offset reductions in total ship numbers.

---

[38] Some publications have stated that the Navy reached a peak of 594 ships at the end of FY1987. This figure, however, is the total number of active ships in the fleet, which is not the same as the total number of battle force ships. The battle force ships figure is the number used in government discussions of the size of the Navy. In recent years, the total number of active ships has been larger than the total number of battle force ships. For example, the Naval History and Heritage Command (formerly the Naval Historical Center) states that as of November 16, 2001, the Navy included a total of 337 active ships, while the Navy states that as of November 19, 2001, the Navy included a total of 317 battle force ships. Comparing the total number of active ships in one year to the total number of battle force ships in another year is thus an apples-to-oranges comparison that in this case overstates the decline since FY1987 in the number of ships in the Navy. As a general rule to avoid potential statistical distortions, comparisons of the number of ships in the Navy over time should use, whenever possible, a single counting method.

Table C-1. Total Number of Ships in the Navy Since FY1948

FYª	Number	FYª	Number	FYª	Number
1948	737	1970	769	1992	466
1949	690	1971	702	1993	435
1950	634	1972	654	1994	391
1951	980	1973	584	1995	373
1952	1,097	1974	512	1996	356
1953	1,122	1975	496	1997	354
1954	1,113	1976	476	1998	333
1955	1,030	1977	464	1999	317
1956	973	1978	468	2000	318
1957	967	1979	471	2001	316
1958	890	1980	477	2002	313
1959	860	1981	490	2003	297
1960	812	1982	513	2004	291
1961	897	1983	514	2005	282
1962	959	1984	524	2006	281
1963	916	1985	541	2007	279
1964	917	1986	556	2008	282
1965	936	1987	568	2009	285
1966	947	1988	565	2010	288
1967	973	1989	566	2011	284
1968	976	1990	547	2012	287
1969	926	1991	526	2013	285

Source: Compiled by CRS using U.S. Navy data. Numbers shown reflect changes over time in the rules specifying which ships count toward the total. Figures for FY1978 and subsequent years reflect the battle force ships counting method, which is the set of counting rules established in the early 1980s for public policy discussions of the size of the Navy.

a.   Data for earlier years in the table may be for the end of the calendar year (or for some other point during the year), rather than for the end of the fiscal year.

Shipbuilding Rate

Table C-2 shows past (FY1982-FY2014) and requested or programmed (FY2015-FY2019) rates of Navy ship procurement.

Table C-2. Battle Force Ships Procured or Requested/Programmed, FY1982-FY2019

(Procured FY1982-FY2014; requested or programmed FY2015-FY2019)

82	83	84	85	86	87	88	89	90	91	92	93	94	95	96	97	98	99	00
17	14	16	19	20	17	15	19	15	11	11	7	4	4	5	4	5	5	6

01	02	03	04	05	06	07	08	09	10	11	12	13	14	15	16	17	18	19
6	6	5	7	8	4a	5a	3a	8	7	10	11b	11c	8	7	8	11	10	8

Source: CRS compilation based on Navy budget data and examination of defense authorization and appropriation committee and conference reports for each fiscal year. The table excludes non-battle force ships that do not count toward the 306-ship goal, such as certain sealift and prepositioning ships operated by the Military Sealift Command and oceanographic ships operated by agencies such as the National Oceanic and Atmospheric Administration (NOAA).

a. The totals shown for FY2006, FY2007, and FY2008, reflect the cancellation two LCSs funded in FY2006, another two LCSs funded in FY2007, and an LCS funded in FY2008.

b. The total shown for FY2012 includes two JHSVs—one that was included in the Navy's FY2012 budget submission, and one that was included in the Army's FY2012 budget submission. Until FY2012, JHSVs were being procured by both the Navy and the Army. The Army was to procure its fifth and final JHSV in FY2012, and this ship was included in the Army's FY2012 budget submission. In May 2011, the Navy and Army signed a Memorandum of Agreement (MOA) transferring the Army's JHSVs to the Navy. In the FY2012 DOD Appropriations Act (Division A of H.R. 2055/P.L. 112-74 of December 23, 2011), the JHSV that was in the Army's FY2012 budget submission was funded through the Shipbuilding and Conversion, Navy (SCN) appropriation account, along with the JHSV that the Navy had included in its FY0212 budget submission. The four JHSVs that were procured through the Army's budget prior to FY2012, however, are *not* included in the annual totals shown in this table.

c. Figure shown does not reflect potential quantity reduction resulting from March 1, 2013, sequester on FY2013 funding.

Author Contact Information

Ronald O'Rourke
Specialist in Naval Affairs
rorourke@crs.loc.gov, 7-7610

www.ingramcontent.com/pod-product-compliance
Lightning Source LLC
Chambersburg PA
CBHW052013280526
45793CB00005B/965